"Many people are aware that the Bible teaches
that sex outside of marriage is wrong, but they are not
always aware of sex that is wrong inside
marriage. This book addresses the issue in a
readable, sensible manner and should prove helpful to
couples whose marriages are less
than God intended in terms of sexuality."

STUART & JILL BRISCOE

"Reading this book was pure pleasure for me—pleasure
over an exciting title, exciting ideas,
even statistics which constantly reinforce the fact
that our God takes pleasure in having created his
children to enjoy every one of his good gifts."

DAVID A. SEAMANDS

Making Your Marriage
a Great Affair

PURE PLEASURE

Bill & Pam Farrel
Jim & Sally Conway

INTERVARSITY PRESS
DOWNERS GROVE, ILLINOIS 60515

InterVarsity Press® is the book-publishing division of InterVarsity Christian Fellowship®, a student movement active on campus at hundreds of universities, colleges and schools of nursing in the United States of America, and a member movement of the International Fellowship of Evangelical Students. For information about local and regional activities, write Public Relations Dept., InterVarsity Christian Fellowship, 6400 Schroeder Rd., P.O. Box 7895, Madison, WI 53707-7895.

All Scripture quotations, unless otherwise indicated, are taken from the HOLY BIBLE, NEW INTERNATIONAL VERSION®. NIV®. Copyright © 1973, 1978, 1984 by International Bible Society. Used by permission of Zondervan Publishing House. All rights reserved.

Cover photograph: The Stock Market/Klaus & Heide Benser

ISBN 0-8308-1637-2

Printed in the United States of America ♻

Library of Congress Cataloging-in-Publication Data

Farrel, Bill, 1959-
    Pure pleasure: making your marriage a great affair/Bill & Pam
Farrel . . . [et al.].
        p.   cm.
    Includes bibliographical references.
    ISBN 0-8308-1637-2
    1. Sex in marriage. 2. Sex—Religious aspects—Christianity.
3. Marriage—Religious aspects—Christianity.   I. Title.
HQ63.F37   1994
646.7'8—dc20   *94-18635*
                                                                          CIP

17	16	15	14	13	12	11	10	9	8	7	6	5	4	3	2	1
08	07	06	05	04	03	02	01	00	99	98	97	96	95	94		

To the sons of Bill and Pam—
Brock, Zachery and Caleb:
You are too young to understand
just how much you gave
so others could find the answers
to the questions
of their hearts.

Introduction

The faces are different, but the words are familiar.

"You are really lucky," said a husband to Bill.

"What do you mean?" Bill asked.

"You and Pam seem to have a really good time."

"You mean on our dates?" Bill probed.

"No. A really good sex life. I sure wish we had that."

His wife, in a moment of vulnerability, approached Pam.

"I feel so alone. I feel used up. I feel like I want to give up on my marriage, yet something inside me says, *no, not yet.* I still love him. I want to be close. I want passion. I want sex to be a pleasurable experience. I want to feel alive and loved."

"If it feels good, do it" has become the dominant philosophy about sex in our culture. But doing it isn't making people feel good. The sexual revolution had a profound effect on the young people of the sixties (baby boomers, born 1944-63), and it continues to affect their children (affectionately known as Generation X).[1]

From 1965 to 1985 teen pregnancies rose 553 percent; sexually transmitted diseases in 15- to 19-year-olds went up 226 percent. Divorce tripled each year from 1963 to 1984; single parent families increased by 160 percent; unmarried couples living together went up 353 percent.[2] The revolution left its mark on those who are adults today, and the next generation will also be deeply affected.

In our (Bill and Pam's) experience in pastoring a church in Southern California, we have found a common frustration among married couples who sincerely desire an intimate relationship. Their previous sexual experience has sabotaged their efforts for a sexually close marriage.

In our decades of marriage counseling, we (Jim and Sally) have met many who share these same dilemmas. As sexual activity outside marriage has increased, so has personal dissatisfaction.

Some have been promiscuous because the philosophy under which they grew up said it was okay. Some have been abused by a relative or date raped by a person who thought any sexual expression was his or her right. Others have been disappointed by the inability of their mate to meet the expectations present-day media have fed us (and we have eagerly swallowed) about an intimate relationship.

Over the years, a burden has developed in our hearts to offer realistic help to these couples. These couples have looked for fulfillment in casual relationships but now have come to the conclusion that maybe marriage will bring hope. They are restless sexually because the philosophy of the sexual revolution taught them that sexual expression was an inalienable right. They have trouble developing and maintaining intimacy because they have never learned the skills that are necessary for a long-lasting intimate relationship.

Our desire in *Pure Pleasure* is to provide practical steps for a couple to practice that will encourage the development of these skills. Our hope is that this will be a practical guide and workbook to empower couples to find the intimacy they are looking for.

We are fellow travelers on the road to marital intimacy. We have learned some key principles about how to build pleasure into an intimate life and want to share our insights to help you on your path toward pleasure.

In the pages of this book, you will meet other fellow travelers. They are people whom we have helped as they walked the road in search of intimacy. They have actively applied the principles that are being presented. We are telling their stories with the hope that you may identify with one or more of them and find in their example the next step you should take on your road. The individuals whose stories are recounted for you in the next chapters are real people, but care has been taken to change details to protect their privacy.

We travelers have been deeply affected by the sexual revolution because we either grew up in it or were raised under its shadow. We were taught that free love and guilt-free sex were a natural and attainable part of life. However, we have also come to the conclusion that the "free" philosophy of the "free-love" movement was not really free. In theory, the sexual revolution was supposed to loosen society's restrictions and provide greater pleasure. Some of that happened; however, the movement also induced a new bondage. A high price has been paid by individuals in their private lives. As a result, we have found the effects to be a mixed bag: the excitement of understanding human sexuality and the nagging disappointment of trying to make sex more than it actually is.

The price paid varies from individual to individual. Some of the true-life tales are just as intense as Steve's story.

A young military man, Steve sat in my (Bill's) office. He'd just stopped by for a minute:

"I got a call yesterday from my wife back home. She says she's tired of marriage. She said she fell in love with an old boyfriend and has been living with him while I've been in basic training. She said marriage is too confining and we should see other people.

"*See other people!!* We're supposed to be *married!* She said maybe when I take a leave in a few weeks we'll go out and have some fun. I don't want fun. I want my wife back! Marriage would be fun to me. I thought we settled this when we said, 'I do!' "

Other true-life experiences are as common as Val and Joel's stable marriage with an extremely boring sex life.

"We don't date. We talk but we aren't close. We have sex but not intimacy," said Val to Sally.

Joel, Val's husband, shared his ideas about sexual intimacy in marriage with Jim:

"Marriage has never been what I thought it would be. It seems Val and I have never really understood each other. I feel like we have sex just for me and Val goes along with it because she loves me. I'm afraid our sex life will always be this way."

Couples like Joel and Val are not necessarily dissatisfied to the point of despair or divorce. But they feel that if God created marriage, romance and sex, there must be more to it than what they experience.

Whether you find yourself confused or bored in your desire for sexual happiness, we are praying you will find practical help for your sexual relationship.

Is This You?

Those born since 1944 have experienced a social upheaval that has affected intimate relationships to their very core. Ask yourself if any of the following characteristics fit you.

☐ You weren't a virgin on your wedding day.

☐ You had more than one sex partner before you were married.

☐ If you have children, you fear they may be affected by AIDS, other sexually transmitted diseases, a crisis pregnancy or severe emotional wounds.

☐ You have difficulty with goals. You may fall into one of two camps: the overachiever who can't decide which goals are best so you try to do them all, or the underachiever who is paralyzed by a pattern of indecisiveness which has your life stalled.

☐ You feel ambivalent toward the institution of marriage, wondering if it can really work for a lifetime.

☐ You have a nagging sense of grief, feelings of loss or lack of trust so you feel lonely even when you are with people.

☐ The lines between helpful sexual material, entertaining material, art and pornography seem blurry to you.

☐ You want your marriage to work but you also want personal fulfillment.

☐ If you are a woman, you have experienced some form of trauma (harassment, rape, molestation, crisis pregnancy or abortion).

☐ You've watched hours and hours of sex or implied sex on TV.

☐ You may or may not have lived together before marriage but you are open to the idea if it seems to make a couple happy.

☐ Divorce (either yours or your parents') has affected your life.

☐ Communication seems to lack the intimacy you thought would be a part of marriage.

☐ You fantasize about a more exciting sex life.

☐ You feel hurt by your spouse's past actions but are uncomfortable talking about it because you don't want to seem judgmental or hypocritical.

☐ You know a lot about sex and intimacy yet feel uncomfortable expressing your own needs and desires.

The sexual revolution kicked the sides out of the morality box.

But as inhibitions escaped, so did the ability to maintain an on-going, pleasurable intimate relationship. There were no handles to help us keep a hold on love. It is our hope that this book can be a "heart hold" so you can experience pure pleasure and make your marriage a great affair.

1
LONGING
FOR
PLEASURE

THE PROFESSOR LEANED AGAINST the chalkboard. The class was almost over. "As you can see," the prof summarized, "medieval chivalry was an unobtainable code of love. It was idealistic romance."

"Yeah, like romance today," groaned Lori as she reflected on the string of empty relationships in her life. She had become cynical from the pain of a broken marriage and a recent desertion by her live-in lover.

"I could have told you romance was dead a long time ago," murmured Karen across the aisle to Lori.

Then the classroom door opened. In walked a handsome man, thirtysomething, holding a bouquet of roses. Lori's heart raced with the hope that maybe her boyfriend had sent these flowers to make up with her. But it was only another disappointment for her as the man confidently walked across the room and placed the dozen roses on his unsuspecting love's desk. He bent over, gently kissed her surprised face and said, "I love you." Then just as quickly he left the room.

The smell of the scarlet flowers perfumed the air. The surprised wife blushed from the overwhelming gesture of love. It was only the second day of the class. These people didn't even know her or her husband. Her heart pounded at the graphic statement of committed love that her daring husband had just made. Her eyes followed her dear one as the door quietly closed behind him. She wrapped her arms around the tender bouquet and quietly sighed.

Questions erupted.

"Is it your anniversary?" asked the startled professor.

"No."

"Your birthday?" asked a newly divorced woman next to her.

"No."

"Then what's the special occasion?" someone shouted from across the room.

"There isn't any. I'm sure he just wanted me to know he loves me," she replied with a confident smile.

The professor, still obviously thrown off by the entrance of the romantic stranger, quickly summed up the lecture and dismissed the class.

The classroom buzzed. Feelings of disbelief, excitement and wonder lingered in the air. As notebooks closed and pencils were stashed away, classmates approached.

"Where'd you get this guy?" Lori and several other women asked after class.

"Where'd he get the guts to do it?" asked some of the men. Many of the group huddled together as they walked down the hallway and to the parking lot, interjecting questions along the way. They all, in their own words, were describing their search for a love that would last.

That evening, with the vase of roses now placed on the night-stand, the couple enjoyed an intense and sexually satisfying time. But that was common to their fourteen-year marriage. We know, because we (Bill and Pam) are that couple.

Now, our love life has not been all roses. Like all couples, we have hit many "transitions," some of them harder than others. One of the hardest was discussing former relationships. We had talked about them some before, but once we were married and sexually active together, both of us became more sensitive to the other's past.

I (Bill) knew Pam had had a string of boyfriends before she met me. Out of insecurity she stacked up boyfriends like trophies of her popularity—sometimes two or three at a time who didn't know about each other.

As she became vulnerable in telling me about them, I felt betrayed. At first, I didn't feel as special as I had in the initial stages of marriage. I felt resentment toward the other men who had touched my wife. Something had been stolen from me, and I mourned. I even found myself angry at Pam for not looking years ahead and saving everything for me.

I (Pam) struggled when Bill described his exposure to some crude sexual experiences in his junior-high days. His friends had made an abandoned shack behind their school into a kind of sexual amusement park: boys would coerce young girls to come for sex while curious friends watched through peepholes. Though Bill used pinball and basketball to escape the peer pressure to participate in the activities inside the shack, he says, "I was exposed to much more than I needed at thirteen!"

Fear welled up in me as Bill told me about the shack, and about a fort he built with a friend, wallpapered with centerfolds, and other things that went on in his teen years. *Our sex life is good now, but what if I get ill, or pregnant, or boring? Will he go*

looking for some of the antics he was exposed to in those years?
My body isn't airbrushed to perfection. How can I live up to those
images?
    Then the anger hit. *How could he? He fooled me! He seemed*
like such a nice guy, but underneath he's just like all the ones I
resented for acting like jerks. In high school and junior college,
I had hated the lewd comments about my body. I hated feeling
forced or pressured sexually. Now I hated the fact that my precious husband could ever have been that kind of guy.
    I wasn't sure of my feelings. I felt panic, nausea, rage, fear and
the desire to get as far away from Bill as I could. Yet I was also
feeling an overwhelming desire to gather him in my arms and tell
him how sorry I was that he had been through all that. My love
was pretty confused for a while. And so was our marriage!

A Love-Hungry World
Today's adults are crying out for a sexual relationship that is intense yet comforting, thrilling yet committed, passionate yet purely
romantic. The top forty music charts are inundated with desires
longing to be fulfilled. Women want a man who is "Shameless"
in his love, "Too Sexy" to be resisted, but committed to going to
"The End of the Road" in devotion. Women expect a guy to give
"Passionate Kisses" yet not create an "Achy, Breaky Heart."
    A man wants a woman who looks at him like he's "Romeo,"
who is "Breathless" at the sight of him. He wants a woman who
will "Lose Control" and get "Dangerous" in giving him "Love
Deluxe."
    Talk shows daily parade people looking for Mr. or Ms. Right.
But even these people have maladies like "Loving Too Much" or
"Fear of Commitment." These same shows often highlight the
newest kink in sex. One guest on the *Jenny Jones* talk show had
sex with the maid of honor from his wedding on the night of his
honeymoon, with his new bride's permission.[1] Sex is everywhere.

Madonna's book *Sex* hit the stands before Christmas 1992 and the publishers were so confident the American people would buy it that they released 800,000 copies.[2]

A *Dateline* special on teens and sex estimated that twelve- and thirteen-year-olds had seen ten years' worth of sex on TV at a rate of 20,000 implied acts a year.[3] One study found that more than 75 percent of televised music videos portrayed visual presentations of sexual intimacy and 81 percent of videos containing violence also included sexual imagery.[4]

Sex sells, and it sells big. The market is glutted with information on sex. So why is it that so many are still longing for an intimate relationship that brings sexual fulfillment and lasting pleasure?

Day in and day out we hear heart cries for intimacy. During counseling sessions and in casual social settings, we listen to the same complaints. "Why can't I find a guy that understands me?" asks a young professional woman.

"My husband just wants to watch TV. I feel like I could stand in front of the TV in a sexy nightgown and he'd just say, 'Honey, can you move over? You're blocking my view,' " complained one wife in her thirties.

"My wife never wants sex anymore. She says she's burned out on it. How can that be? She's only in her thirties!" exclaimed a professional man.

"Date! What's that?" moaned a mother of two.

"My husband is always looking at other women. I wished he'd look at me the same way he does the swimsuit edition of *Sports Illustrated!*" a beautiful newlywed in her twenties chimed in.

"Our sex life is so predictable. If I don't get some excitement, I'll go looking somewhere else. I love my wife and kids, but this life is a bore!" moaned a young father.

"Nobody loves nobody anymore. There's no respect, no trust," says Cilly Acevedo, 19, of the Bronx.[5] Many students (66 percent of girls, 42 percent of boys) interviewed said that being grabbed, groped, talked to explicitly was "just a part of school life." Girls interviewed had given up on relationships. Many of the young males interviewed rationalized group assaults. They were wary of "looking soft" to their male peers if they had a relationship with a girl rather than just sexually harassing her.[6]

If you were born after 1944, you have lived under the influence of the sexual revolution. The experimentation and free expression of sexual activity during the late sixties and seventies have produced a generation of Americans who are destroying their opportunities for sexual fulfillment and a lifetime of intimacy. Their questions tell the depth of the problem.

Why Can't I Find Love That Lasts?
Today people are migrating from partner to partner, looking for the love and intimacy they desperately want. In spite of the fear of AIDS, the average person in the U.S. has increasingly more sex partners per year. In 1988, 67 percent of sexually active women from ages 15 to 54 had more than one sex partner in a year and 41 percent had more than four.[7]

John Marchese, a writer for *Mademoiselle* magazine, confessed to breaking a heart in a short-term live-in relationship of a few months. "It was just around the time we were beginning to plan a winter vacation to someplace warm that I walked out one night and never called again."[8]

"Some of us make a career out of putting off commitment," says *Twentysomething* author Steven Gibb. "The marriage-for-life ideal is being replaced by the serial monogamy we see all around us."[9] The trend is startling. Monogamy is defined as serial live-in relationships that have been redefined as long-term if they pass the three-month mark.[10]

One set of researchers proposes, "It is quite possible that women and men often do prefer a monogamous relationship, with one sexual partner, even if it is without the traditional obligations and responsibilities of marriage."[11]

Men, in particular, seem to take advantage of this "no strings attached" approach to relationships. Twenty-five percent have had at least five sexual partners in the last year.[12]

But serial non-marital sex is not providing the lasting pleasure that is so longed for in our society. Millions are still yearning for that magical love that will last all their lives.

Having More Sex but Enjoying It Less

Maggie, a young mom in her late twenties, remarks, "Sometimes at night I dream of leaving Matt for my first lover. Evan was so sweet and romantic. I wonder what life would be like with him. He was much more attentive than Matt is. Or Randy, the musician I lived with one summer. He wrote songs for me and would sing them after we'd make love. When I remember all my lovers, Matt seems so boring. He's a great dad for the kids, but the fire and thrill just aren't there anymore.

"I actually saw one of my old boyfriends while I was out shopping the other day," Maggie continued. "We had coffee. I gave him my phone number. I don't know if I am more excited or scared. What if he really does call?"

Serial sexuality is beginning at younger ages, but has only *increased dissatisfaction.* Women who first had sex when they were teenagers reported two to three times as many partners as those who were in their twenties when they first had sex.[13] One study revealed that those who experienced intercourse at fifteen or younger were least likely to rate their marriage and marital sex as good.[14]

As couples get more frustrated with their sex lives, they may go looking for a thrill. One in three married men and one in four women have had an affair.[15] People are having more sex but *less* lasting pleasure.

Sex therapists interviewed for *Newsweek* reported 50 percent of patients experienced inhibited sexual desire.[16] Sexual problems and emotional stress are on the rise. The greater number of sexual partners seems to be causing deeper frustrations. In fact, 10 percent of lovers found romantic relationships so painful that they hoped to never love again.[17]

Why Didn't Living Together Divorce-Proof Our Marriage?
To avoid divorce, some couples experiment with trial cohabitation. Many see this as a screening process to test whether a person can bring them lifelong pleasure. However, living together and marriage commitment are as different as reading about how to scuba dive and actually going into the water and trusting your breathing equipment.

One fallout of cohabitation prior to marriage is the stark difference of marriage survival after the "I do." A total of 35 percent of couples who cohabit will divorce before their fifteenth anniversary compared with 19 percent who didn't cohabit.[18]

In a University of Chicago study, researchers found that people with a more tentative commitment toward marriage were more likely to cohabit. Cohabitation itself "produces attitudes and values which increase the probability of divorce."[19] People are short-circuiting their own lasting pleasure for a moment's pleasure in serial sexual relationships.

Why Do I Feel So Lonely?
Kara dropped into the couch. In an exasperated tone she sighed, "I don't know if I'm in love with Jason or if I'm just afraid of being alone. I've been married before and it is *awful.* But being alone is awful too. I just can't decide which is worse —being in a marriage where I feel alone even if he's there, or not being married and feeling alone with no one there. Even if a guy stays for the night, the crumpled sheets in the

morning remind me of my lonely heart."

In those under thirty, 75 percent have had premarital sex, and 20 percent have had sex with a married person.[20] Yet all of this sex isn't creating closer relationships. Just the opposite. Researcher George Barna declares that "more than any prior generation, they feel estranged from God, separated from each other, lacking meaning in life, void of roots and societal connection."[21]

Frank Haycock and Patricia Garwood, authors of *Hidden Bedroom Partners,* suggest that single people often have sex just to avoid going home alone. They note that "a couple can also go through all the physical intimacies of intercourse and still remain emotional strangers."[22]

But people don't want to remain strangers. They want to know and be known. They desire an intense relationship that leads to intimate lifelong pleasure. Tragically, though, 61 percent believe that most adults will divorce within the first five years of marriage.[23]

It seems everyone is still looking for that one relationship that will give sexual and emotional pleasure, but there is a widespread fear it may never happen.

Where Can I Find Lasting Pleasure?
Catherine Johnson, author of *Lucky in Love,* interviewed 100 couples who saw themselves as happy and asked the secret of their happiness. Dr. Johnson determined that "happy couples strongly believe in and practice monogamy. For them, being faithful to each other was not what made them happy, it was what made the marriage possible in the first place." She adds, "Marital fidelity is the 'of course' of marriage; happiness comes from the good qualities couples build for themselves upon that foundation."[24]

The commitment controversy rages on. Is marriage necessary for a pleasurable sexual relationship? In the sixties, a revolution rose to debunk the notion of marriage as a reliable institution for sexual satisfaction. Since then, we've been living with the disastrous fallout.

However, the four authors of this book believe the concept of commitment is not an unreasonable drag on a relationship. Instead it is the rallying point for lasting sexual fulfillment and intimate companionship!

Liz and Jared were both children of broken homes. They were in love, but they kept procrastinating when it came to tying the knot. As they sat in the counseling session, their faces were a mix of hopeful anticipation and cynical dread. "We're in love now, but we're afraid it won't last," said Jared.

His young love nodded her head in agreement. Liz added, "We don't want to become a statistic. There has to be a way to make it last, right?"

There Is Hope!

Maybe you're like Liz and Jared. You have been told there are erogenous zones, catalogs of sex toys, G-spots and methods for safe sex. Perhaps you are daily fed the message, "Go for it! Do whatever makes you feel good! Live for today! Don't worry, be happy!" You may desperately desire a happy-ever-after romance but are told that kind of love is a fairy tale. You have arrived at a sexual *pressure point*, but not a *pleasure point*.

There is hope! You can turn pressure points into lasting love and intimacy by following the practical "pleasure points" at the end of each chapter of this book. The principles are simple to understand . . . but challenging to implement.

Some of the exercises are to improve verbal communication, to help you express your desires and feelings. Others are action oriented to help enhance your romantic and sexual life. Reading is not enough. Putting action to the theory makes all the difference. Most of the exercises can be adapted if only one spouse is interested in improving the marriage. Some of the chapters will be helpful to those who are engaged or seriously dating, but most are intended to provide lasting pleasure within the context of marriage.

You're on the road to sexual pleasure. Each chapter is a sign-post, pointing the way to a lasting love life.

Pleasure Point:

During a quiet conversation alone with the one you love, discuss this quick quiz. Each of you select a road symbol from the list below. Then tell each other what feelings about your sex life you are trying to communicate with the road symbol you have chosen.

Stop Sign
Wrong Way/Do Not Enter
Yield
Detour Ahead
Road Closed
Freeway Entrance
Green Light
Rest Area
Vista Point

The symbol that best describes my sex life is _____
because _____ .

2

THE
PLEASURE
OF
COMMITMENT

GREG, YOU HAVE *GOT* TO MAKE A decision!" Terri insisted. "I don't want to spend the rest of my life waiting for you to take a risk. Do you want to get married or not?"

"I want to marry you, Terri, but I'm still scared." Greg then nervously ventured, "Do you think we could get engaged now and tie the knot in a couple of years?"

"Two years! Anything can happen in two years. I love you, Greg, but I want to get on with my life. I don't want to live in limbo any longer."

Greg could feel his pulse race. The exhilaration of marrying Terri was mixed with the fear of making such a big commitment. He wasn't sure he wanted to get married, but he was sure he wanted to be with Terri . . . so he decided he should take the big step.

He didn't ask Terri immediately, but he did start to scheme how he would propose. He planned a date for them where they would end up at their favorite lakeside spot. They had spent hours talking by the big oak tree that stretched out over the quiet waters of the lake. It was there they had discussed their goals, dreams and desires.

Amidst the fragrance of fresh grass and the blanket of wild meadow flowers, they had both shared their desire to have three kids and own their own business. They had dreamed about owning a boat they could use on this lake that had become such a fond part of their love.

Once they got to the lake, Greg led Terri to the shade under the oak tree. He gently guided her to the big round log that lay nestled in the grass. A spot on the log had the bark rubbed off and formed a perfect seat. Greg was noticeably nervous. His moist hands and parched mouth betrayed the anxiety he had worked so hard to disguise.

At first Terri didn't understand why Greg was so agitated. But when Greg bent down on one knee in the cool grass, Terri's heart awoke. Her pulse quickened. Her eyes sparkled as tears of joy filled her eyes.

As Greg looked into Terri's eyes from his crouched position, he felt a tidal wave of emotion run through him. If he committed to Terri, there would be no turning back. If he didn't commit to Terri, he would regret it the rest of his life. He stared at her for what seemed like hours as his desire to be with her wore down his fear of commitment.

Greg could feel the last paralyzing effect of fear subside as he took the leap of commitment and said, "Terri, will you marry me?"

Terri looked long into his eyes—and said an enthusiastic yes.

Greg pondered for a moment how empty his life would have been if he had let this opportunity slip away.

Growing Up Hopeless

Greg and Terri almost didn't make it to that day, because for most of his life Greg had not thought marriage was good for anyone. His parents divorced when he was eight. His childhood was divided between two separate lives.

Life at his dad's house was relaxed and full of material things. He had his own phone, television, stereo and all the clothes he could wear in a lifetime. He enjoyed freedom but felt a sense of loneliness as his dad seemed interested only in competing with his mom for the best parent award.

He often tried to drown out the sounds of his dad and his new girlfriend having sex in the bedroom next to his, but the stereo couldn't blare loud enough to cover up the moans or relieve the anger raging inside him. *Why didn't Dad love Mom like that?* he thought.

Life at his mom's house was structured and orderly. He had to share the phone with the rest of the family. He watched the family TV. The whole family was on a strict budget. His mom made a lot of statements about character being more important than money. It seemed to Greg that his mom was trying to convince him she was better than his dad.

Greg resented his parents' competition. The only person who seemed to understand was Holly, a girl from school who was also trapped, bouncing between her two parents each week. Greg loved talking for hours with Holly.

But talking soon turned into petting and petting into regular sex. Greg was disillusioned when the talking he'd found so healing changed. Now the goal of the relationship was only to find secret places and times for sex. Sex became as lonely for him as his vain attempts to use his stereo to forget his parents' failed marriage.

Is Marriage Good for Anyone?

The ache in Greg's heart when he and Holly broke up pushed him to conclude, "I don't ever want to get married. It hurts everybody involved, especially the kids."

Greg was able to deny that he wanted to get married until he met Terri at work. Their professional conversations were intellectually stimulating, so it didn't take long for them to turn into personal conversations. Terri seemed to understand Greg, and he thought maybe he had a chance to actually be happy with her. After dating for almost a year, Greg was anxious to discuss a further commitment.

"Terri, I have never known anyone else like you. I think we might have something special going here. What do you think?"

Terri replied, "I love you, Greg. Our relationship is very special to me and I think it has real possibilities."

Greg felt his heart rate quicken and his courage rise with her reassurance. "How do two people go about being happy together?" he asked her. "I'm scared I'll do the same thing my parents have done.

"What do you think it takes to be compatible? I have heard other people say that we should make sure we are sexually compatible before we think about something as important as marriage. That sounds pretty smart to me. How about you?"

"I don't know—that's a pretty big step," Terri interjected. "I've had sex with a couple other guys. We seemed compatible but it didn't make those relationships work.

"One of those guys actually said to me, 'It must be right for us to be together because it felt so right when we did it.' Well, where is he now? We gradually grew apart after we started having sex, instead of growing closer. I left the relationship with the feeling that I had been conquered and was no longer interesting. I don't want that to happen to us."

Testing Sexual Compatibility

The last three decades have been a time of trial and error in the search for intimacy and partnership in life. It has been assumed by our society that sexual compatibility is one of the major sources of stability in marriage. While it is true that men and women who reported being satisfied with their sexual relationships also reported being satisfied with their marriages,[1] it is not true that good sex before marriage necessarily leads to a good marriage. In fact, recent evidence points out that premature sexual activity catapults intimacy into confusion.

Our society has fooled itself into thinking it is in love because it is having sex! Research is plentiful indicating that sexual arousal produces romantic attraction.[2] In other words, if you are aroused while spending time with someone of the opposite sex, you will conclude that you are starting to fall in love with that person. You will most likely decide to further the relationship, believing you are made for each other.

In the short run, the thrill of an emotionally charged, sexually passionate relationship is seductive. In the long run, however, *sex without committed love is agonizingly destructive to the relationship.*

It appears that the main criterion for deciding the extent and value of sexual involvement is the emotional commitment of the couple. One researcher uncovered that "the more emotionally involved a person was in a relationship, the more likely increasing levels of intimacy were regarded as appropriate."[3]

Confusion results from the fact that females quite often attribute a higher level of commitment to a relationship than do males.[4] According to a study of college students, males expect sexual intimacy sooner. Females tend to tie sexual intimacy to love and commitment (dating one person only). The presence of love appears to justify sexual intimacy for females. In any given relationship, the male may perceive that the couple is at a lower commitment level than the female. Because of this misperception, women give sex to receive the love they think is already present in the relationship, while men give love to encourage more sexual activity.[5]

This pattern of emotional misunderstanding between the genders is repeated over and over. With every misunderstanding comes a new emotional wound. A *Redbook* magazine survey revealed that those who experienced intercourse by age fifteen or younger had more sexual partners in their lives and were more likely to rate their marriage and marital sex as bad.[6]

In another study, it was found that 54 percent of college students had some sexual experience with another child prior to adolescence, and 85 percent had a sexual experience with another teen by age sixteen. If childhood genital contact had taken place, subjects were more likely to have engaged in premarital intercourse during young adulthood and had more intercourse partners than subjects with nongenital childhood experiences.[7]

Breakup rates for those who have sex before marriage are alarmingly high. The intimate nature of sex makes the termination of a relationship traumatic for two reasons:

1. Repeated hurts from repeated breakups with sexual partners can erect a wall around the heart that isolates the individual from intimacy.

2. An individual can become emotionally hooked into a negative relationship because of the sexual involvement.

The authors of *Why Wait?* tell us, "Sex forms an almost unexplainable bond. It locks people into relationships. The longer it goes on, the harder it is to break it off."[8]

The implication is that sexual arousal can lead to "feeling in love," which can lead to sexual activity before marriage. This premarital experience can be a bombshell that explodes your chance at a lifetime of sexual compatibility. This happens because one or both of the partners may develop nagging doubts about whether he or she has chosen the right partner. Doubts linger as each wonders whether the marriage happened because of true love or because the heat of the moment had them trapped.

On the other hand, sexual purity can lead to greater passion and pleasure for a lifetime. Tim and Beverly LaHaye, in a survey of over 3,000 people, found that wives who had experienced no premarital sex experienced greater marital sexual satisfaction than did those who had experienced sex prior to marriage.[9]

Does Cohabitation Guarantee Success?

Let's go back to Greg and Terri. After talking with Terri about sexual compatibility, Greg concluded that sex without any commitment would not work for them. He didn't want to lose Terri but he was still scared of the idea of marriage. A lot of his friends were living with their girlfriends, so he thought he would ask her to live with him.

"Terri, what do you think about us moving in together? It seems like a good idea to me. You know, my parents didn't do too well together. Maybe they never would have married if they had tried it out first."

"Do you want to get married or not, Greg? It sounds like you want us to live together so we can prove we won't make it as a married couple."

"That's not what I mean," Greg interrupted. "At least, I don't think that's what I mean. I am just too scared to even think about marriage or putting any kids through the same junk I went through."

Terri responded, "I think I would like living with you, but most of the people I know who are living together right now aren't doing so well. They always seem to be fighting over stupid things like whose house it is or who paid for the toothpaste last time. Or they're living separate lives and just sharing the same bed.

"Or they're waiting for some magical moment when it will be

right to get married. When I ask them when that time will be, they don't know. I want more out of life than that. I want to feel that I belong to someone and he belongs to me."

Terri was intuitively sensing what is becoming obvious in current research. The next logical step after sexual involvement is cohabitation. Couples decide to move in together—to try being married before they get married.

In a study reported in *Adolescence*, 24 percent of males and 18 percent of females actually cohabited. But astoundingly, 71 percent of the males in that study and 68 percent of the females were totally open to cohabitation.[10]

Those who cohabit honestly believe that this gives them an opportunity to practice marriage without any strings attached. In theory it seems plausible, but recent studies have shown that those who cohabited before marriage are almost twice as likely to end their marriage before the fifteenth anniversary as those who didn't cohabit.[11]

The underlying fear that drives people to live together is fear as to whether this marriage can work. Living together, it is reasoned, gives an opportunity to practice being a couple while not fully giving of themselves emotionally, sexually or socially. The results are often devastating to the couple.

First, there is a loss of respect. Each partner recognizes that the other does not value the relationship enough to stick it out if it gets difficult. The growing conclusion is, I am not worth very much to this person. If life with me gets inconvenient, I will be left very quickly.

Second, there is a loss of trust. If the relationship is going well, life seems good. But if the relationship is not going well, a deep and agonizing sense of loss paralyzes the individual with fear, anger, confusion and a host of other self-defeating emotions.

One study found that cohabiting women were more jealous than married women, and they had a high emotional dependency on the male live-in partner. Many developed a pattern of few friendships, no job advancement aspirations and few outside interests.[12]

Even after a cohabiting couple gets married, the same fears linger. Many people are nagged by the thought that the other partner could leave at any time. They are plagued by the possibility that since they drifted into commitment, they could just as easily drift out. Others are driven by fear to please or placate a spouse even if it violates personal values. They just don't want to capsize the rocking boat.

Third, there is a loss of accomplishment. The present moves at a relentless pace into the future. Everyone makes life decisions and sets future goals to keep up with the demands of maturity and aging. When the decision is made to live with someone without being married, the individual puts off the biggest relationship decision of life. They each continue, however, to make vocational, economic and spiritual decisions that affect the rest of life. A future decision, to either get married or split up, will profoundly affect all the other decisions made independently of each other. The person who decides to cohabit adds to the stress level of his or her life because so many permanent decisions continue to be made in the midst of a temporary relationship.

One part of life, the marriage decision, is trapped in indecision. But the rest of life moves forward. Cohabitation, unlike marriage, puts off key life decisions—children, buying a house, establishing family traditions. Cohabiting couples do not truly intermingle possessions and lives to become "us," because this arrangement may not work out.

Does Eliminating Commitment Guarantee Success?

Terri was sensing that Greg was getting very serious about her. The more interested he became, the more confident she felt to discuss their future. A couple of months after Greg and Terri's conversation about cohabitation Terri asked, "Greg, what do you think about marriage? You and me—husband and wife? Mr. and Mrs. Greg Johnson?"

"I don't know," Greg said with a halting voice. "You know I never wanted to get married. My parents were an awful couple and all my friends are either getting divorced or complaining about how unreasonable their wives are. I just don't know if we will ruin our great relationship by getting married."

Marriage itself is being redefined. Too often it's commitment without commitment. Modern marriage vows have been rewritten to say "as long as we both shall love," giving the couple the opportunity to peacefully dissolve if the feeling should one day disappear.

When asked to define what a family is, 28 percent of Generation X (those born after the baby boom) said it was "people you have a close relationship with." Logically, if the closeness wanes, the family dissolves. Another 25 percent said it was a "mutual commitment." So if one partner wants to flake on his or her vows—no more marriage.

An additional 24 percent said it was compatibility. Therefore, if the couple experiences growth and change as individuals and for a period their interests seem incompatible, the marriage is null and void.

Another 11 percent said a family is simply people who live together. That would mean that when one partner is absent due to business responsibilities, illness or military duty, the vows lose their meaning.

Researcher George Barna helps explain why this generation is so susceptible to this short-sighted thinking about marriage. A total of 65 percent agree that the purpose of life is enjoyment and personal fulfillment. Of those surveyed, 59 percent agree that the first responsibility in life is to oneself and 74 percent say that one should not let marriage limit opportunities and activities in life.[13] Marriage is, therefore, a useful tool as long as it leads to fulfillment, but if it becomes hard work it can be discarded.

The sacrifices necessary for maintaining a vital marriage are nearly impossible if one is constantly looking out for oneself. Some people think a mate is extremely valuable when he or she is making you feel good about yourself and supporting you in your life pursuits. However, when your mate requires you to support him or her, rather than allowing you to accomplish your own goals, the relationship becomes an unattractive hindrance to your first responsibility—yourself.

Today's generation wants many relationships because friendship and companionship are considered to be very important. The success of these relationships is sabotaged, however, because of a general fear of any type of long-term commitment. People consistently enter into relationships, but when the commitment necessary to make a relationship work becomes uncomfortable, they bail!

Those who want to be committed in relationships run into another roadblock. That is, the person who is loved doesn't believe the love is real. We have been trained by the past to believe that significant relationships don't last. All around us, marriages fall apart and families split up. Stepfamilies don't survive and families are further scattered. Close friends often move away so our long-term friendships evaporate.

As a result, we have a hard time believing that lasting relationships are possible. The most important people in our lives are always auditioning for a place in our heart.

Tragically, the will to fight for what is most valuable has never been developed. Researchers support this thesis by saying that this generation seems "to lack the emotional stability and endurance to withstand a battle of wills and ideas."[14]

Marriage attitudes today are summed up by the woman who handed her husband divorce papers accompanied by the statement, "I am sorry I lied when I said for better or for worse."[15]

Is There a Happily Ever After?

Years later, Greg and Terri returned to their favorite lake for their anniversary. With joy and pride, they towed the sailboat they had managed to acquire. As they backed it down to the water, Greg looked at Terri and said, "Are you ready to go?"

Terri, looking strangely preoccupied, did not answer. Greg asked, "Terri, are you all right?"

"I was just thinking about the call I got from Andrea before we left. She and Jake are calling it quits after six years. It seems as if so many of our friends have lost their marriages.

"Thank you, Greg, for working through the major issues of commitment with me before we got married. We have a good marriage, don't we?"

"We sure do, Terri. Let's launch the boat."

As Greg and Terri sailed around the lake, they passed the spot where Greg had proposed. Terri and Greg quietly thanked God that he had given them the courage to be committed.

Pleasure Point:

Stand face to face at the foot of your bed. Take turns renewing your wedding vows aloud. Use your exact vows or this sample ceremony, personalizing with your mate's name in the blanks.

Husband: I, _____, take you, _____, to be my lawfully wedded wife, to have and to hold from this day forward. I promise to love you, comfort you, honor you, and forsaking all others, cling only to you as long as I live.

Wife: I, _____, take you, _____, to be my lawfully wedded husband, to have and to hold from this day forward. I promise to love you, comfort you, honor you, and forsaking all others, cling only to you as long as I live.

3
THE
PLEASURE
OF BEING
UNDERSTOOD

PETER SAT DAYDREAMING AT HIS desk, remembering how often he and Kristi used to have sex. He had been shocked into reality last night when she exclaimed, "I never really have liked sex!" Her heart seemed so calloused when she said those words.

When he had begun the conversation about their sex life last night, he was honestly wanting to discover what had happened to their relationship. It had been weeks since they had sex and he longed for her body. Her continual resistance was making him confused and angry. But her words drained the hope out of his heart. She seemed to pull the plug on the possibility of any future intimate fulfillment.

*Our marriage had such possibilities and now she is ruining it!
Or maybe I am ruining it? I don't know, maybe it just isn't worth
it anymore.* Peter buried his head in his hands, wondering if there
was any way out of this.

The Fear of Sexual Incompatibility

To try to find some answers to his dilemma, Peter invited Bill out
to lunch.

"Thanks for having lunch with me today, Bill. I needed to talk
to someone. I feel I can trust you. I am afraid that Kristi and I are
becoming incompatible sexually."

"You think you are sexually incompatible?"

"Yeah, I get the feeling she doesn't even like sex. We used to
have good sex, and she even liked it—at least, I think she liked
it. But she doesn't seem to anymore. I don't know. I am so
confused about this."

"What makes you think she doesn't like sex anymore?"

"She doesn't want to try the things I want to try. And she never
initiates lovemaking. I would like her to be more aggressive,
more interested, more enthusiastic. Instead, she seems bored. I
feel like she would be satisfied if we never had sex again."

"Have you talked with Kristi about this?"

"I've tried, but I never get anywhere with her."

Spectator to Your Own Love Life

Kristi knew that she had wounded Peter, but she had been hurting for so long that it didn't matter. It wasn't that she didn't like
sex, but Peter's version of sex didn't even hint at meeting her
needs. She was so tired of feeling like a spectator in her own bed.

She wanted to talk with someone about this, but she didn't
want any of her friends to know. She had heard Pam speak at a
seminar and thought she might have some insight. Maybe a talk
over lunch with Pam would give her hope.

Kristi very bluntly poured out her complaints to Pam:

"Peter seems so obsessed with sex. He is only interested in me when he wants to make love. I wish he would take time to get to know me and what I want, rather than just push me into doing what he wants. I don't know if two people can become sexually wrong for each other, but it feels like it might be happening to us."

Pam gently asked, "Well, have you talked to Peter about this?"

"I've tried, but I can't get anywhere with him. He only wants his own way!"

Coming from Different Directions

Peter and Kristi are caught in a classic struggle between men and women that has intensified in the last three decades. Psychologists are starting to establish that men and women define intimacy differently. "Women derive intimacy from talking face-to-face; men often obtain emotional closeness from doing things side-by-side, like watching and playing sports."[1]

Peter and Kristi's generation has been led down a path that magnifies the difference between the sexes rather than taking advantage of it. Both men and women are told they can get what they want. Men view sex as a recreational activity, while women view sex as a way of being loved.

The end result is predictable. The wife is not recreational enough for the husband's desires, and the husband is not verbal enough for the wife's desires. Adding to this dilemma, other specialists have noted that "women tend to shut down when they are unfulfilled sexually and men tend to feel more sexual hunger with lack of fulfillment."[2] Both partners wind up empty and start looking for options they believe will better meet their needs.

The answer is found in communication. Sex is a relationship, not an event. If an intimate relationship is to endure, the couple must learn to share openly, honestly—but gently—with each other.

Kristi said frankly, "Peter, we need to talk about what is happening to us. I love you, but I feel that you *never* really care about me as a person. When we make love, you are *always* in such a hurry. You *never* take time to meet my needs."

Peter responded, "I am not *always* in a hurry, Kristi. Just because you are bored with sex doesn't mean I don't want to have it anymore."

Even though Peter and Kristi were speaking honestly with each other, they also needed softness. Crucial principles need to be followed to create a relationship of emotional closeness and lasting love.

Be Specific

The words *never* and *always* stifle communication like screwing the top back on a bottle of soda while it is fizzing. These broad generalizations rarely work because:

1. They are a lie. Phrases like "You are always in a hurry" and "You never take time to meet my needs" cannot be proved. An exceptional example of one person meeting the other's needs can always be found.

If you took your car to a mechanic who said, "This car doesn't work," you would ask, "What is wrong with it?" If he responded, "This car has *never* been in good working order," you would know immediately he was wrong. You would think, *Either this guy is really mean or he's in the wrong profession and should look for a new job.* Unfortunately, we make ridiculous statements about the overall condition of our marriages when all that is needed are a few specific adjustments.

2. There is no constructive way to respond. A wife who hears her husband say "You never have liked sex with me" has no way to respond, except to deny the allegations. It is nearly impossible to move toward middle ground in the argument.

Generalizations paint your mate into a corner, encouraging

defensive reactions. In our (Jim and Sally's) extensive experience with married couples, we have found that the stalemate can be broken if you give your mate the benefit of positive regard. Phrases such as "I prize you" or "I value you" tell your spouse that he or she is so valuable to you that it's worth working through the tough times.

Positive regard was found to be *the most significant attitude* in a study which explored communication within marriage.[3] If you value your spouse, you won't set him or her up for a no-win response to your generalization.

3. The generalization is not the real issue. When a wife says, "You have never really loved me," she may be trying to say, "I don't feel that you love me. Last night I felt you used me to satisfy your needs but didn't take my needs into consideration." In order to respond to one another and make adjustments in the relationship, specific complaints, not generalizations, need to be worked on.

Communication is disclosure to yourself as well as disclosure to your spouse.[4] First try to figure out your real feelings and admit them to yourself. Then choose specific words to express those feelings to your loved one.

Be Tenacious

Peter and Kristi figured their marriage was valuable enough to try this conversation again.

Peter ventured, "Kristi, I'm sorry I reacted negatively to our conversation yesterday. Can we try it again?"

"Sure. Let me see if I can get my feelings out in a way that won't hurt. Peter, I want you to know that I love you, but I am concerned that our intimate life is in trouble. The last three times we made love, I felt as if you were in a such a hurry to satisfy yourself that my needs were not considered."

"What did I do the last three times that is so different from our first two years together?" Peter asked.

"Well," Kristi responded, "it just seemed that sex was over before I was really ready. You didn't spend time kissing my neck, caressing my body or talking with me affectionately. It was as if we were just exercising."

Peter then spoke more openly than he ever had before about sex. "There are times when sex is just fun, not necessarily romantic for me. I don't always feel like taking the time to make it satisfying for you. In fact, if I could plan our sex life I would make it about 50 percent quick sex and 50 percent slow and emotionally intimate."

"Fifty percent!!" Kristi exclaimed. "How can you trivialize something so intimate by reducing it to just messing around! Sometimes I think you are more of an animal than a man!"

Permission Granted

Kristi was short-circuiting Peter's attempt to share his side of the situation. People want to be open and intimate with one another, but they are often afraid to trust others, even those with whom they should feel secure. As a result, people must constantly give one another permission to share a little more of themselves. The process of giving permission consists of clues given to one another that say we really do care and that we are not going to judge. Ways to give permission to open up are:

1. Repeat a key phrase the other person has just spoken.

2. Rephrase an idea in your own words and then ask, "Is that what you are trying to say?"

3. When your mate says something that surprises you, don't react with disgust, shock or judgmental statements.

Peter and Kristi need to practice being more gentle with one another. They can either be offended by the other's initial complaints and build a wall between themselves or they can give each other permission to keep sharing until they understand one another. Understanding transports couples to new levels of intimacy.

Resolving Hurt Feelings

The wrinkling of Peter's face revealed the hurt he felt. Kristi's accusation of his being an "animal" stung him. Staring at the floor, he replied, "That really hurts. To think that you see me as an animal is depressing. I thought you liked it when we had sex."

Kristi was taken back by the hurt in Peter's face. She really thought he had stopped caring and was just looking at her as a sex object rather than a life partner. The look of anguish softened her heart and made her think that maybe there was hope.

She continued, "I'm sorry for calling you an animal. I guess I just got my feelings hurt because you seemed to be ignoring my desires in our sex life. Rather than talking with me, you just tried new things. Don't get me wrong, I liked some of the new things we experienced—but I missed you. I missed talking with you, understanding you, having you understand me. I want to share all of life with you, not just play with you."

Peter appreciated the response but felt some subtle pressure to always meet Kristi's needs, so he took this opportunity to add, "Kristi, let me see if I understand. For you, sex is a very intimate experience. If you could have your way, every time the experience would last at least an hour and would be attended with flowers, dancing, romantic conversation and lots of affection. Is that right?"

"Yes! I would love that."

"Well, how do you feel when it isn't like that, because I don't always want it to be long and drawn out. A lot of times I like it to just be fun and short."

"Sometimes I like it when it is fast too. But when it is fast too often, I feel like I'm having sex just to please you and it starts to seem impersonal. Peter, do you like it when sex is impersonal?"

"Kristi, that's not fair. I don't think making love is impersonal. I just think we are different. I am afraid we may becoming incompatible."

"That's a pretty strong statement, Peter. It scares me to hear you say that."

Permission to Struggle

Peter and Kristi are not unique in their struggle to find their identity as an intimate couple; couples like these are an epidemic. Undoubtedly, many of you reading this can relate to Peter and Kristi all too well. How can intimacy be developed that is satisfying to both partners?

Give yourselves permission to struggle. We live in a world inundated with various philosophies about intimacy and sexual relationships. An ocean of sexual material challenges our thinking. Some of these philosophies teach that male needs must be met, whether or not the wife's are met. The dominant media culture portrays most sexual activity as short, exciting, active and intense.

Some philosophies encourage women to focus solely on their needs. A backlash in the dominant media culture is crashing in waves upon women's thinking. It overemphasizes independence from men and promotes superiority over men.

Although our generation has been strongly encouraged to be self-centered and fiercely independent, we lack comparable information on how to be a truly happy married couple. Because of the constant indoctrination on personal rights, multiple partners and the high divorce rate, great pressure is on the couple who wants to be permanently passionate partners.

Enjoy Your Uniqueness

Courageously protect your relationship as a unique creation of unimaginable possibilities. It is our experience in counseling that most couples settle for what they have been told they should experience in terms of intimacy, pleasure and partnership. Rather than explore their uniqueness as a couple through courageous communication, they settle into a rut consistent with the culture around them. This is not what marriage was created to be.

Marriage is designed to be a dynamic, growing pursuit of unity between two people who are very different from one another, yet who each have what the other needs. Discovering the uniqueness inherent in your relationship requires vulnerability in expressing who you really are to your mate. Share the good qualities that make you a wonderful person as well as the dark secrets of your heart. Share the pleasure and distinctives of being either male or female.

A wife must understand that her husband does not understand her. He does not and cannot experience what it means to be a woman, and he will never know unless he is told.

A husband must understand that his wife does not understand him. She does not and cannot experience what it means to be a man, and she will never know unless she is told.

Listen Carefully

Be a tenacious listener. If you seek to communicate about intimate details of your life, you will often feel uncomfortable. You may feel offended or sense that the situation cannot work. This happens because we are slow communicators. Some do not verbalize thoughts quickly or succinctly. Others talk quickly but hide their real feelings in a barrage of conversation so the meaning is still hidden. Our emotions need to warm up to intimacy and vulnerability.

The more we perceive that the person we are talking with genuinely cares, the more willing we will be to share what we really think and feel. This is never more important than when we are discussing our sexual, romantic needs. To help your listening be more effective try these steps:

☐ *Create positive eye contact.* Don't stare through your mate or intimidate him or her with a piercing look. On the other hand, don't look away from your spouse either.

□ *Use encouraging body language.* Lean forward. Hold hands. Sit comfortably. Smile at your mate.

□ *Pick up on key phrases.* Repeating a phrase encourages fuller disclosure from your spouse. If your mate says, "I am scared to be really open with you," respond with, "You are scared if you open up to me?" If you have positive eye contact and encouraging body language, your partner should respond by giving more information such as, "Yes, I am afraid that if I tell you what I really want, you will reject me."

□ *Rephrase the thoughts of your spouse.* This shows that you are tracking with him or her. "I sense you are uncomfortable talking about our intimate relationship. It sounds to me as if you are afraid I will think you're unreasonable or that I will reject you. Is that what you are thinking?" Statements like these are extremely helpful to encourage your mate to be more open with you.

□ *Try gentleness.* The generation we live in is so obsessed with sex that there is an entire slang language just to refer to the various sexual acts of which humans are capable. We are more attracted to the slang terms than we are to the technical or affectionate names for body parts and sexual activity.

The result is that we dehumanize human life and make it more like mating than lovemaking. We also reduce each other to bodies to be used for sex. We demote the act of sex to a performance that can be played out by any two people, rather than seeing sex as a means for couples to seek to unify their whole lives. By using language from the heart rather than slang terminology, sex is elevated and personalized.

(Note: If you need more help with the skills of communication, we recommend Jim's book *Making Real Friends in a Phony World.*[5])

Be Gently Honest

Peter and Kristi took these suggestions to heart and reinitiated their conversation about their intimate life. Each of them set time aside to think through what they liked in terms of sexual expression. They then got together at a nonsexual time and place and began sharing how each viewed their sexual relationship. They took time to describe how they liked to be touched, kissed, talked to and loved.

They tenaciously listened to each other and encouraged disclosure at a level that was new for them as a couple. They were free to discuss these issues at length because there was no pressure to engage in sexual activity. They were able to digest and process the information that was shared before they began incorporating the new ideas into their relationship.

Don't give up on your marriage! Just like Peter and Kristi, you can get to know each other better than you ever thought possible. If you are willing to be gently honest with your mate about your needs and listen to the honest needs of your spouse, you will begin to discover that the possibilities of your love for one another are unlimited.

Pleasure Point:

Plan a nonsexual encounter for the purpose of discussing the level of intimacy in your relationship. Prior to this meeting, write out your thoughts in note form, a poem, a song or whatever format works for you.

Take turns sharing what you do and don't enjoy in your romantic experiences. Get to know as much as you can about what brings pleasure to your mate.

Ask questions like:

What are your fantasies?

What do I do that you like?

What would you like us as a couple to try together?

4

THE
PLEASURE
OF LOVE
UNDER PRESSURE

Y OU DON'T THINK WHAT I DO IS important!" shouted Amy to her husband as he entered their condo. "You say, 'I support you,' but when it comes right down to it, you bail!"

"That's unfair, Amy. You know the pressure is on me to perform at work. I have to put in the extra hours. It's expected. Besides, my job is paying most of the bills!" said Darrin defensively.

"Oh, that's really fair. I didn't throw my paycheck up in your face when you were in grad school. We made a commitment to each other. You'd finish your degree and I'd work full time, then I'd finish my degree while you worked in your new career. You aren't keeping your end of the bargain."

"Well, we didn't have Emily then."

"She's your daughter too. I just need you to be a father to her."

"Oh, now I'm a bad dad too!" Darrin raised his voice and threw his hands up in desperation.

"Shhh. Don't wake the baby. *I* just got her to sleep," Amy stated, emphasizing the "I."

"Amy, I do care."

"I need you to show that you care," Amy pleaded. "My plate is full. Working part time, caring for Emily and going to school is killing me. I need some help!"

Amy paused for a moment, then renewed the attack. "That's not to mention keeping the house up. We've both slacked off on the deal we struck there." She nervously checked her watch. "Darrin, I can't argue anymore now. I'm already late for class because you got home late. Talk to you later."

Amy walked out the door and yelled back over her shoulder, "You're on your own for dinner."

Darrin plopped down in the nearest chair. He ran the scene over in his head and thought, *I'm always on my own for dinner. Except when Emily is awake, then I have her to feed too. I miss Amy but she makes me so mad. She's gotten so pushy and demanding. I'm trying my best to keep up my end of the bargain. I just never counted on the stress. There's so much responsibility. Why can't she give a little?*

As Amy drove to the university, she fumed to herself, *Darrin used to seem so sensitive. I remember when he wanted to make my dreams come true—to make our dreams come true. I'm just so tired. I miss Darrin but he makes me mad. He's gotten so pushy and demanding. I'm trying my best to keep up my end of the bargain. I just never counted on the stress. There's so much responsibility. Why can't he give a little?*

Impatient for the Dream

Today's adults want it all. And they want it right now! Those under forty claim their right to a nice home, two successful and fulfilling careers, financial freedom and happy, well-adjusted children with whom they spend wonderful quality time.

It is a psychology of entitlement, says author Daniel Y. Yankelovich: "What other generations have thought of as privileges, the baby boomers [think of as] rights."[1] A harsh reality hits when the economy and their own human time limitations don't cooperate with their idealism.

Many twenty- to forty-year-olds now feel as if they are in the fast lane with no exit ramps. The stress of the race causes couples to become impatient with each other. They truly desire to meet each other's needs, but trouble arises when their personal expectations collide with their spouses' expectations and their children's needs.

Superwoman Meets Kryptonite

The societal forces since World War II have laid the groundwork for many unrealistic expectations. Women were told they could have it all. They could have a perfect husband who would love them perfectly, perfect children, a perfectly wonderful marriage, a perfectly successful career, perfect friendships, a perfectly clean house—and a perfectly trim figure as well. They were given a host of promises that they thought would surely bring perfection to their life. But now they are just *perfectly tired!*

Women's seminars and study courses still promote the rights of women to have freedom from reproduction by birth control and abortion. Birth control was a welcome relief to many married women when it was introduced; however, its relief soon spread to the single sector as well. Widespread birth control practiced among singles led to the mistaken idea that sex outside the context of marriage was now free from consequences. The consequences merely went underground, popping up at inopportune times in a variety of masks. One of those masks is the illusionary belief that women can have total autonomy over choices about their lives.

Women are taught that they are free to pursue the career of their choice and free to explore a variety of relationships—heterosexual, homosexual, parenthood without a man, freedom from parenthood at all. Women have had this underlying belief pattern woven into them by the feminist revolution. A little voice screams, "You don't have to be bound by your husband. Children will hold you back from reaching your potential. Don't let anyone tell you what to do! You are a feminist!"

In *Second Stage*, Betty Friedan lists quotes from young, radical women who are struggling to forge a picture of femininity apart from marriage and family.[2] One woman thought of a "fetus as a parasite" and motherhood as "a condition of terminal psychological and social decay, total self-abnegation and physical deterioration."[3] Even as late as 1986, women's journals featured writers like Sheila Cronan who said, "Marriage constitutes slavery for women; it is clear that the women's movement must concentrate on attacking this institution."[4] Even Friedan commented that women are "for the first time in history freed from passive, necessary submission to their role as breeders of the race."[5]

Come a Long Way, Baby?

Even though many of these messages come from the farthest end of the women's movement, the underlying theme is widespread: *Perfect success comes when you do exactly what YOU want!*

Three decades of women have been told that fulfillment of personal goals other than marriage and family is the primary avenue to individual success. It's been a thirty-year tightrope walk for women trying to balance their roles. If relationships with men or children stand in the way of achieving a dream, it is understandable to simply abandon the relationship and pick up a less demanding one.

Women have made great strides in many fields and have been recognized for tremendous contributions. But deep in the heart of many women, unfulfilled desires for marriage and family pull strong on their heartstrings. Women are engaged in a tug of war, with career pulling on one end of their heartstrings while love for husband and family pull at the other. You may be one of those women.

Feelings of guilt and a nagging sense of loss may linger deep in the back of your mind as an insatiable loneliness presses deep into the farthest corner of your heart. You may feel like many who are haunted by this subtle pressure to be perfect in all arenas simultaneously. You may say in exasperation, *I must be Superwoman to survive!* But Superwoman has grown tired of trying to have it all. The fast lane is an impersonal place. After all the battle, even Friedan notes, "The equality we fought for isn't liveable, isn't workable, isn't comfortable."[6]

One nearly thirty-year-old married woman put it this way, "I feel like I'm being forced to choose, and with either choice, I'm losing."[7]

You may feel cornered by the decision of what you are going to do with your life. You lash out, even at the one you love most, in an attempt to save your identity. You may tenaciously hang onto your goal, even if it causes marital conflict, because you fear that if you lose your goal, you lose yourself.

Clark Kent Climbs the Corporate Ladder

This secure-your-goals-at-all-costs agenda is by no means a purely feminist platform. Men have been praised for their "focus" everywhere from the boardroom to the Superbowl. Headlines across America praised 1993 Superbowl coach Jimmy Johnson for his dedication to the game of football, which included divorcing his wife to concentrate on building a winning football team.[8]

One CEO, interviewed for an article entitled "100 Most Successful Executives," stated that he got into the top ten by total commitment. "Reaching the level of business success that I have requires total commitment. If your family is too demanding, get a new family. That's what I did."[9]

Most men are not on the list of the 100 most successful executives, and most men don't want to use their families as a down payment on their success. However, many men are confused over just what their role is today.

Such confusion has spawned a new men's movement to help men get in touch with their feelings. This movement is an attempt on the part of men to express their frustration with not being able to have it all. Men are saying that they are feeling the stress of not being able to focus. Demands on a man in the workplace have not diminished. Added to the workload are the new equally shared household responsibilities. Men in these circumstances often lash out at their spouse, fearing failure if they split their energy between work and home.

Seeing the writing on the wall, a whole segment of society is turning its back on the superman/superwoman model. These men and women are seeking to restore sanity, balance and intimacy to their lives.

One woman in her early thirties, familiar with the climb up the corporate ladder, said, "We have to get away from this. It's crazy. We have to slow down—somehow! I'm not sure how. Move away? Maybe to the country? I just know we never see each other. When we do, we fight. In my heart I know we're fighting for the same thing—us!"

As card-carrying members of our yuppie, type-A, overachieving generation, Bill and I (Pam) find this struggle to balance it all is an ever-present battle for us. Sometimes we join forces to wrestle with our schedules. At other times we use our daily calendars as weapons against each other. In my mind, competing fears battle for control. *Am I spending enough time with our three boys, both in quality and quantity? I'm working so much with Bill—is that going to affect us as lovers? Will being on this mommy track permanently sidetrack my career choice? In ten years will I regret the decisions I am making today?*

We have a magnet on our refrigerator that says, "I was made for someone who welcomes a challenge." I bought it for Bill as a thank-you for working with me as I struggle with these questions. Several years ago, I turned my internal battle on Bill and began to fight him for my every goal. In turn he began to battle me for time as well. Overall, our marriage was good, often passionate, but a wall was rising between us. We struggled to pinpoint its cause through numerous discussion sessions. Each of us felt this wall growing brick by brick. But the recurring tension between us made it obvious we still hadn't found the tool to knock it down.

One night, right in the middle of a heated discussion, we both looked at each other and said, "We have to pray—*now!*" We fell to our knees. Neither one of us wanted to talk to God or each other, but we did it anyway. We held hands, not because we wanted to but because we knew we had to join hands as a symbol of goodwill, just as boxers touch gloves at the end of a fight. As we each poured out the ugliness and frustrations that were locked inside, we began to see the pattern that had been battering our marriage—*we didn't trust one another!*

We had always prided ourselves on the amount of trust we had in our marriage. I knew Bill was on my side; he was my biggest fan. Bill had often bragged about how much he had accomplished personally and professionally because I had been such a cheerleader for him. It shocked us that the subtle battle in our own minds to "have it all" had stripped us of the ability to believe that the other wanted the best for *both* of us. We threw up the white flags and began to talk again, this time in calm conversation. Together we have been prying individual bricks out of the wall that had been keeping us apart.

A New Plan for Us
How does a couple re-create marital intimacy when the schedule has made virtual strangers out of once romantic lovers? Men and women need to accept the seasons of life. Earning a Ph.D., raising three kids, owning a four-bedroom home, a cottage on the lake and a ski boat, and being chairman of the board of a multinational corporation aren't accomplished in a three-year period of life. We need to relax and enjoy accomplishing different goals in the various seasons of life. As couples, we may even want to rethink whether some of the traditional material goals are desirable for ourselves and our families or will distract us from more important things.

Couples need to replace the "I" with "we" and incorporate their personal agendas into a unified lifelong family plan. This pattern must include a patient look at a "couple process" rather than a panicked race to meet independent goals.

Over a period of several days, Bill and I realized that we needed to step back and take a good, hard look at where we were and where we wanted to be. As we were driving home from a ministry obligation, Bill pulled the car to the side of the road. The lights of the city lay quiet and calm ahead of us, a stark contrast to the frothing discontentment rising in each of our hearts.

"Pam, I love you—I want you to know that right from the start. I can't keep going like this."

"Me either," I said as tears welled up in my eyes. "We need a break. I can't even see things clearly anymore. Sometimes I battle for things that I know shouldn't be that important to me."

"And I take all your obligations and goals as a personal insult— like you don't want to spend time with me."

"Oh, I love spending time with you. A lot of what I do is for you—or at least I thought it was."

As the conversation continued, Bill and I talked of conversations he had had over lunch with Jim. Having lunch with Jim had reminded Bill of how life has many seasons, some of which are very strenuous.

Bill had heard all the theory in his seminary class with Jim, and I had read Jim and Sally's *Women in Mid-Life Crisis.* We knew all the information. Some of Sally's words shouted from the back of my mind as Bill and I talked. "You are a unique woman and God has a plan for you."[10] I knew I wanted Bill in the center of that plan. And I knew he wanted me in his plan. We needed to rediscover *our* plan. We knew there were answers to this transition, but we needed a plan to redirect our life.

"Bill, we need to get away, together, and really deal with this." And we began to arrange for three days on our own in a quiet place where nobody knew us. Those days proved wonderfully significant and healing.

Get Away
Here is a plan that will help the process work in your relationship. To make optimum use of a time away, plan on at least forty-eight hours. Each spouse needs to do some individual thinking ahead of time.

☐ *Set a date.* Discuss the idea of when and where to get away. It's not to be a sightseeing tour; it's a time to renew your love. The place should include a room for rest, relaxation and privacy. It is also helpful to have quiet places to walk. The beach, a lake or a mountain setting is nice. Most couples feel less intimidated sharing their feelings on a walk rather than at a face-to-face glare down.

You should clearly decide who will make the reservations, pack, arrange for child care—and what kind of budget you have to work with. Include in the budget a small amount for the Pleasure Point listed at the end of this chapter. Keep in mind that this time away is an investment in your future, so it is worth every penny you can spare.

If you are in desperate financial straits, this may be a time to call in some favors. You may be able to housesit for a vacationing couple, borrow a motor home or trade homes with a relative or friend.

If time off is a total impossibility and all your spendable income went into buying this book, then a "plan B getaway" can be accomplished at home. But you must be very disciplined. Arrange for the kids to spend the weekend with friends or relatives. Treat your home as if it were a time-share condo. Housework and yard work are off limits because you are a guest!

Here are two exercises each of you should do beforehand. If that's not possible, spend an hour alone early in the weekend, each personally thinking through issues in preparation for conversation as a couple.

□ *Write your life goals.* Ask yourself what you want written on your tombstone. It might help to list a phrase that captures your hopes for each of the following areas:

Spiritual life
Marriage
Children
Work
Community
Extended family
Finances

Spell out where you see yourself in each of these areas in the next five to seven years. Evaluate how far you have to go to bridge the chasm between today's life and your hopes and dreams for the next few years.

Mark the areas you feel will be volatile when you share these dreams with your spouse. To check for selfish motives, think about a few thought-provoking questions such as:

Will this issue matter in twenty years?

Will my children be affected now? when they are grown?

In the face of eternity, could I stand before God and justify this item as being motivated out of love?

Will this issue benefit those who will cry at my funeral?

Question your willingness to sacrifice. Are you willing to slow down or scale back in order to come to peace in each area? You may want to consider several options. But to be successful, you need to be willing to keep all your hopes, dreams and plans on the bargaining table. Negotiation has to be a major part of your vocabulary.

☐ *List your activities and priorities.* On 3 x 5 cards, include anything that takes your time and energy. Mark the cards so you know which are greater priorities to you and thus are less negotiable. In later conversations around the bargaining table, the cards become tangible ways to shuffle two lives together into one livable stack.

Get Rest

When you actually arrive on the getaway, *rest first.*

Bill shared his feelings about the retreat after sleeping in on the first morning, "I didn't even like you at that point, because just thinking about our life made me tired. I was on the verge of complete exhaustion. After a good night's sleep, I felt like I was human enough to talk."

Next, plan to eat well. "Let's both have our favorite breakfast, then walk around the lake and pray," I suggested to Bill.

Ask God to help. If one spouse is uncomfortable praying, the other may offer to pray a simple prayer such as, "God, help us. We love each other and we want to make this work. Give us both words of love today."

Louis Evans, a former pastor of the Hollywood Presbyterian Church, said that he never knew a couple who divorced after praying together, on their knees, every day for a week.[11]

Swiss psychiatrist Paul Tournier writes that "when each of the marriage partners seeks quietly before God to see his own faults, recognizes his sin and asks forgiveness of the other, marital problems are no more. . . . They learn to be absolutely honest with each other."[12]

Prayer had been and is the key that Bill and I use to unlock conflict so we can deal with it and destroy it. Often, praying will help us see areas of imperfection in our own lives as well as misconceptions about God. Prayer and reading the Bible remind us that God is on our side in this battle for marital happiness.

Get Busy
Find a place to talk freely where you both can share on each subject. Use the skills discussed in chapter 3, "The Pleasure of Being Understood," to ensure that the conversation doesn't become inflamed by old, fruitless communication patterns. Try to address the issues, not attack your partner.

In severely estranged relationships, marital counseling can serve to lance the boils and let all the built-up resentment and hostility escape. A counseling office can be a neutral setting where new communication wounds can be kept to a minimum and old scars can heal. Some couples may need a few sessions with a counselor before they will be ready for a private getaway.

To maintain an intimate atmosphere, take breaks to walk, lie out in the sun together or eat. Use the cards you both made to negotiate back and forth until you can create a workable plan where you both agree on the same agenda.

Write down any plans or ideas you come up with. Spell everything out on paper so you'll have a decision-making guide for the future. The conversations should draw you closer together, so you may feel compelled to make love.

On the getaway, or within a few days following, review the conversations about your deepest aspirations and dreams. Try to remember why they seemed important. Put yourself in each other's place. How would you feel if the dream you longed to see fulfilled ebbed away?

Give a Gift

Over the next few days, after you get home, shop for a small token or symbol of the dream you think is most precious to your spouse. If you are really at a loss, choose a gift that validates him or her as a person. In athletics, each player studies a playbook so when a specific play is called the team will work in unity to achieve the goal. You two are a team, and this process of "getting on the same page" of life's playbook is a cause for celebration. So plan a special evening to give your gifts to each other. Let us (Pam and Bill) give you a glimpse into the evening of gift giving that we shared.

I opened the large flat box Bill handed me. I found a beautiful briefcase. Inside the case were several small packages. A small card on the first one read, "I believe in you." Inside was a gift certificate for me to order business cards for the home-based business I wanted to start when the semester ended.

The next gift was slightly larger and it had a note that read, "I believe in us." Inside was a daytime organizer with red hearts marking "Date with Bill" once every week for the first month. A specially marked weekend was noted with the message "See package three." Package three was a brochure for a place I had said I'd love to go "next time we get away." One tiny package remained—a picture of Bill and the boys with a card that read, "Thanks for all the time you spend making us a family."

I handed Bill his gifts. There were five different colored envelopes, each containing a card. The first card contained the recipe for Bill's favorite meal and a note that said, "My heart has been away from home but I want to sit at our candlelit table and share this with you. It's in the freezer. You pick the day and time."

Card two contained a few certificates to a driving range. "You gave up golf to spend more time with me and the boys. We want to come watch you practice."

Card three was a handmade coupon for an evening of Monday night football without distractions.

Card four was attached to a box containing a tie and a Post-it note that said, "For those power lunches."

The last card contained a poem describing our time away on the getaway, including references to how much I enjoyed intimacy with Bill.

I said quietly, "Thanks, Bill. Thanks for listening and believing in me. I love you."

Bill leaned across, lightly kissed me and whispered, "Thanks, Angel. I really did miss you. You're the best."

Later that evening, as we walked hand in hand toward our bedroom, I said, "Thanks for being patient with me through all this stress."

Bill smiled and nodded, "Pam, thanks for your patient love toward me."

We have discovered, just as you will, that "love does not consist in gazing at each other but in looking together in the same direction."[13]

Pleasure Point:
Just like Pam and Bill, we all need tangible reminders that our mate is on our team. Each choose a gift or symbol to encourage one goal or dream which your spouse has shared. Remember that the amount of money you pay is not nearly as important as the amount of time you spend choosing just the right gift that says, "I'm your biggest fan!"

Now plan a special quiet moment alone to exchange your gifts.

5
THE PLEASURE OF FORGIVENESS

JENNIFER LAY IN THE BED SEETHING. She played the picture over again and again in her mind. She couldn't believe that someone she loved so much could have done the things Matt had just described to her. She was glad the room was dark. She knew her face would have betrayed her true feelings.

The thought of her husband forcing himself on another woman sickened her. The victim's cries for help seemed to echo in her ears. That woman's pleadings to stop were bouncing off their bedroom walls.

Matt had violated that woman's trust. Date rape seemed too kind a term for the aggressive assault. The fact that he had been a teen didn't salve the wound. Matt's confession and grief over his actions didn't bandage the gaping hole in Jennifer's heart. She knew the victim's life had never been the same after that night long ago. Now she wondered if her life would ever be the same after this night.

Jennifer had managed to voice a reassuring no when her husband had asked, "Will it make any difference to you now that you know?" But it *had* made a difference. She stared into the blanket of darkness. She felt so alone. She hadn't even known him when the events had happened, yet she felt betrayed. He reached out for her. She pretended she was asleep, but sleep wouldn't come.

What's Going On with Us?

Betrayal, confusion and anger are just a few of the many feelings that may be carried into a relationship as a result of past indiscretions. The now-adult children of the sexual revolution have grown up with the notion that to be happy they have to be able to express themselves freely—sexually and otherwise.

While it is well documented that a healthy sex life contributes to overall marital satisfaction,[1] this generation has taken sexual gratification a step further. One researcher concluded, "In no past society known to me has sexual fulfillment been elevated to such preeminence in the list of human aspirations. If the Declaration of Independence were revised today, total sexual fulfillment would have to be added to the list of inalienable rights."[2]

This philosophy has manifested itself in provocative clothing, provocative entertainment and provocative sexual behavior. It is rare to find individuals in this generation who have not had some sexual experience outside a monogamous marital relationship. Stories of experimentation with promiscuity, *ménage à trois*, sadomasochism, homosexuality, orgy-type behavior and the like are commonplace. It appears there are no restrictions to the types of sexual behavior in which our society will indulge. This is only a façade, though. A national survey revealed that the American people do in fact have a sense of conservative morality.[3]

Bad Decisions—Poor Judgment

When two people from the post-revolution generation decide to get married, they often have to work through their feelings about their spouse's previous sexual encounters. They also often need to work through their feelings about how their own choices in the past are affecting the current relationship.

John and Becky came for help after they had been married for about a year. It was a second marriage for both of them and Becky had three kids from her previous relationship. Becky first married when she was very young because she was pregnant and the father seemed like a nice enough guy. The outdoor wedding was filled with flowers and birds and the good wishes of friends. But things changed quickly after the wedding. Her first husband became more demanding sexually and had outbursts of violence and physical abuse toward Becky. She stuck with him for six years. But the day he swung at their three kids with a shovel was the day she decided to get out.

John was there when Becky needed help. Since Becky and the kids needed a place to stay, it seemed like a noble thing for him to offer his house. John had grown up in a very permissive home and believed sex was a good thing to be freely shared by consenting adults. He had been involved in his share of group sex activities. The two abortions he had paid for left him no room to judge Becky for the choices she had made in life.

Becky didn't like the fact that John had paid for abortions and John didn't like the abuse Becky had allowed to happen, but it seemed as if living together might give them both a new start. For a while they lived together like roommates, but eventually a romance budded and after a year they married.

The Emotional Legacy

Past sexual experiences can bring emotional baggage into any relationship. The legacy of the post-revolution generation is choices made for the purpose of self-gratification. Often these choices have left you or others wounded. There is a nagging frustration that there's no way to go back and undo it. However, the key to unlocking the future of your relationship lies in the ability to forgive the past.

Giving and receiving forgiveness is a delicate process because it requires a high level of vulnerability. You must be willing to open yourself to rejection and disappointment as you grow toward the possibility of a new level of intimacy. Following are two of the steps we have found to be vital in the process of experiencing forgiveness in a marriage relationship.

1. Forgiveness begins by admitting that something wrong has been done by either you or your spouse. Being upset over experiences from the past will rob your present relationship of its intimacy. Evaluate the situation that troubles you to determine if an error was actually committed. If something wrong was done, you have identified an area that needs forgiveness.

2. If a transgression was experienced, release yourself or your spouse from responsibility he or she can no longer do anything about. Forgiveness in marriage includes seeing and acknowledging an offense, then saying to the person, "I won't require you to make up for this, because I know you can't."

If you withhold forgiveness, the aching in your heart will swell. In the area of sexual intimacy, you may even feel as if every sexual partner from the past is coming to bed with you, unless you totally forgive each other.

If, on the other hand, you conclude that nothing wrong was done, then you need to talk about it in enough depth so that the pain goes away. You may need professional counseling help to resolve some past memories.

Forgiveness That Doesn't Work

Watch for these common errors that couples make when extending forgiveness to one another. If you find yourself making one of these errors, back up and rethink what you are saying, then try again.

1. Just mouthing the words. Saying, "Please forgive me" or "I forgive you" and not meaning it is an attempt to run away from the issue. Your words may say, "I forgive you," but your actions say, "I don't."

2. Making a blanket statement. Saying, "If I've done anything wrong, forgive me," is an attempt to sweep the past under the rug all at once. Instead of examining the debris and choosing how to dispose of it, this method simply has the two of you walking around on a lumpy rug. Issues need to be identified. Be specific in identifying offenses so your mate knows what is to be forgiven. But don't relive every situation in vivid detail and inflict greater pain on your partner.

3. Minimizing the pain. When a person asks for forgiveness, don't say, "Oh, it's okay." It's not okay. There was an offense committed that needs to be acknowledged and forgiven. I (Jim) am frequently guilty of saying, "It's okay, forget about it." I'm really denying that the problem ever existed rather than granting forgiveness. I'm learning to say, "Yes, I forgive you."

4. Justifying the offense. Phrases like "I didn't know any better then," "I'm a different person now," "Everybody else was doing it," or "That's in the past" are attempts to duck responsibility. Nothing is truly in the past until it has been forgiven. Until then, it is as if the suspenseful music from a horror show is playing in the background of your life—the villain can attack at any unexpected moment.

Deciding to Forgive

As John and Becky were considering whether or not to marry,

they figured a marriage to each other would be much better than Becky's terrible relationship with her first husband. John loved Becky, so it surprised him when the thought of raising her ex-husband's kids was repulsive to him. He sensed a growing coldness toward Becky as his thoughts ran wild inside him:

How could she have been so stupid as to fall in love with such a jerk? Why was she so out of control that she married a guy like that? Now I have to face him every other weekend and help raise his kids. The thought of her having sex with him sends me up a wall! Why didn't she save herself for me?

John felt that Becky had been wrong when she married her first husband, but he believed that she had the right to make her own choices. *When she decided to marry, she was doing what made her happy at the time.*

John wondered what right he had to say that Becky had done wrong. How could he say that her kids were the result of a mistake? The turmoil in his mind was oppressive. He was desperate to get rid of his feelings of disgust. John needed to forgive Becky for her past actions and all the results.

Becky also needed to forgive John for his promiscuous past.

As John shared his frustration over Becky's previous marriage, she felt anger well up in her heart. Her thoughts ran wild too: *At least I kept my kids. John wasn't man enough back then to take on the responsibility of a parent. Instead he tried to run away from the consequences by paying for two abortions. How can he be so strong in condemning my past when his is just as bad—maybe worse!*

Embrace the Truth

The essence of forgiveness lies in facing the truth. All of us have made wrong decisions which hurt us and those closest to us. The thrill of the moment overshadows the long-term consequences. The rational decision-making process is clouded by the rush of passion. The line between positive and negative choices becomes blurred. A decision is made—but the pain of that decision is often slow in coming. When the fallout hits, couples must be prepared to bind the wounds that threaten to tear apart their love.

If a couple will admit to themselves that they have made some wrong choices, they can forgive themselves and then offer forgiveness to each other.

John and Becky decided they wanted to be free to love one another completely, so they began exploring the process of forgiveness in counseling. They each wrote two lists. The first list was entitled *The Things I Have Done for Which I Ask Your Forgiveness.* The second list was entitled *The Things You Have Done Which I Forgive.* After being shown the technique in a counseling session, they set aside an evening alone and began sharing their lists and their feelings.

Asking for Forgiveness

"John, please forgive me for choosing a mate who was abusive to me and my children."

"Sure, Becky, I forgive you for deciding to have three children with a man who was a terrible husband and father."

Becky reacted sharply, "I don't like the way that sounds. Do you think the children were mistakes, like they never should have been born?"

"No, that's not what I mean. What I mean is that when you realized what a poor role model your husband was, you should have stopped having kids with him."

"So it was okay to have Jennifer, but Bobbie and Jim are mistakes?" Becky retorted.

"No, I love your kids. I think they are all very special! Let me see if I can start over.

"I think that God was very good to give you the children. They are turning out to be great kids. I only wish they could have been my kids. I wish they hadn't had to experience your husband's abuse."

Becky softened, "I have often felt the same way too. I love my kids and I would do anything for them—I would die for them! I wish I could have had these kids without all the turmoil. I wish I had done it differently, but I still want my kids!"

"That's why this is so difficult to talk about," John responded. "Your kids are great and I love being their dad. But it's just hard to deal with their living every other weekend with a man who is so bad for them. Things would be a lot easier if God had given us the same kids without all the complications."

"But without all the complications we wouldn't have these kids," Becky replied. "They would be different kids. And I love *these* kids, even though their father is a creep."

"I know, Becky. And I want to stop holding this against you. I know it won't be easy and we may need to have this conversation again, but I am deciding today to forgive you. I love you!"

Wrestling with Forgiveness

John took a turn next and decided to approach the subject of the abortions he had paid for in the past.

"Becky, please forgive me for the actions in my past that led me to pay for two abortions."

"I think I can forgive you for that," Becky said hesitatingly.

John squirmed in his seat. He secretly hoped Becky would allow this to be dealt with quickly. But he wasn't very satisfied with her response, so he answered, "You don't sound too sure about forgiving me. It sounds like you want to forgive me, but that you are not really ready."

"You're right," responded Becky. "I am not really ready to forgive you but I know I should. I know what it is like to be pregnant at a difficult time in life—yet I kept my children. To me, life is so precious that abortion is out of the question."

John bristled with frustration and blurted out, "So do you think life is not important to me? I'm not proud of what of I did. Looking back, I wish I had never paid for the abortions. But I can't go back and change it."

The frustration in John's eyes captured Becky's attention. She wished she could just let go of her anger. But she didn't really understand. She probed for more information by asking, "I know you feel different today, but why were you willing to do that back then?"

"I don't know, Becky. I really didn't think about it. I wasn't having sex because I wanted a committed relationship. I was having sex because I wanted to have sex—it felt good. The thought of being a parent scared me. I was afraid I would be a horrible parent and the child would pay the price for the rest of his life. It seemed like the right thing to do at the time."

"Do you still think it was right?" Becky probed.

"No, Becky. I have told you before that I am not proud of my past. I wish I had done things differently. I wish I knew those two kids, especially now that I know your kids. I wish I could make the whole issue go away."

"I can tell this hurts you, John, but I'm not sure I am quite ready to let it go. It still scares me to think you might have pressured me to abort my kids if we had been together back then."

John became visibly upset and blurted out, "I can't believe you would hold this against me. I was so young and I think I've proved myself with your kids."

The conversation ended abruptly with both John and Becky hurt and frustrated.

Leaping over the Edge

We have often found this type of reaction to be typical when a couple is sharing in a vulnerable way. The point of vulnerability can be like being told you need to leap over the edge of cliff.

It can be scary! But with the right equipment the jump can be exhilarating.

I (Bill) remember the first time I practiced rappelling. I had on a full-body harness with a rope attached at my back. I was instructed to jump off a platform that was about forty feet above the ground. I was told the man at the bottom would control the rope so that I would be gently lowered down to the ground. As I looked over the edge of the platform, my heart raced and my fears rose to the point of choking me, but my determination pushed me not to chicken out.

The jump was one of the scariest things I have done. I did a swan dive off the edge as terror mixed with a shot of naked exhilaration shot through my body. I tried to be stoic—but my fear caused me to let out a scream that is still echoing in the mountains.

Looking back, the experience has become one of my best memories. I pushed past the point of fear and experienced the thrill of conquering a new barrier. In the same way, when you as a couple push past the point of fear in being vulnerable with one another, you will experience the exhilaration of true intimacy.

John and Becky got back together to resume their conversation. Step by step they were able to work through the tension caused by their hurt feelings. They have continued to sincerely work through these lists with one another. At times a great deal of tension rises between them as the vulnerability reaches uncomfortable levels. But they also experience a great deal of pleasure as their vulnerability draws them together as one.

The Source of Forgiveness

Most couples bury past indiscretions and lifestyle choices. These choices are never confronted or talked about. If they are discussed, real feelings are either masked in a veil of false concern for the happiness of the other or used to batter one another in a barrage of criticism.

Couples struggle over how to gauge the vulnerability and forgiveness in their marriage. They have no answers to questions such as: How do we know for sure what we need to forgive? Where do we get the strength to forgive?

We believe that Christianity is a great source of encouragement in this area of marriage. Forgiveness is one of the major tenets of the Bible's presentation of how to have a personal relationship with God. The details of this presentation are presented in the last chapter of this book. But it is important to realize here that God himself follows the two steps we are encouraging you to take in offering forgiveness.

First, God recognizes that we have all done things that are wrong. The Bible says, "We all have wandered away like sheep. Each of us has gone his own way."[4] God knew we would disappoint each other. He knew we would seek to fulfill our own needs and desires at the expense of others. He knew the free will he gave to human beings could be used to choose harmful lifestyles as well as healthy ones. Rather than explain this away, he boldly admits that he is aware of our shortcomings. But he doesn't stop there.

God then goes on to release us from the burden of having to make up for the wrong we have done when we receive his forgiveness. He has declared, "They will get to know me by being kindly forgiven with the slate of their sin forever wiped clean."[5] As a result, "we're a free people—free of the penalties and punishments chocked up by all our misdeeds. And not just barely free, either. Abundantly free!"[6]

Your ability to forgive will become a reality and your healing will begin as you accept God's forgiveness of you. As you experience God's willingness to forgive all your mistakes, you will gain the ability and desire to forgive your mate's personal offenses. When you choose to exercise your heart's desire and forgive, that is the point where your pleasure can begin. As you give and receive forgiveness with your spouse, peace enters your relationship.

Pleasure Point:

Each of you make two lists. Title the first list *The Things I Have Done for Which I Ask Your Forgiveness*. Title the second list *The Things You Have Done Which I Forgive*. Sit face to face on your bed and verbally share each item with your spouse. Do not progress to the next item on the list until forgiveness has been extended and received.

We suggest you follow these guidelines as you share your lists with one another:

1. Be specific.

2. Don't glamourize past mistakes.

3. Don't elaborate the details of the past. Long, in-depth descriptions may rip deeper wounds.

4. Names probably aren't necessary unless they are already known by both of you.

For example:

Do say: Please forgive me for choosing to have sex before I met you.

Don't say: Please forgive me for the petting I did with John. Forgive me for the twelve times I slept with Harry. Forgive me for going to Cabo San Lucas with Spencer and Sun Valley with Mark.

Definitely don't say: Forgive me for thinking George was a better lover because he brought me flowers, and bought me this beautiful necklace and was very good in bed, especially the way he . . .

When your conversation is finished, tear up the lists into confetti. Celebrate your forgiveness and your newfound freedom to love without limits.

6

THE
PLEASURE
OF
FAITHFULNESS

Tiffany stared out the frosted window into the dark night. Although I (Pam) was in the room, she could have been speaking to anyone or no one at all. "Hank doesn't know—I never want him to," said Tiffany. "It was just a couple of nights, that's all. But I guess if I were honest with myself, I loved the attention Rick gave me. Hank just seemed so into his job. When he was at home he was always studying. There didn't seem to be any room for me anymore."

Tiffany turned slowly toward me. But when our eyes met, she promptly walked over to her dressing table and reached for her brush. Gazing blankly into the mirror, she methodically brushed through her thick locks as she continued, "At work, Rick would tell me how great I looked, he'd listen to my ideas in meetings, he was so encouraging about my career . . ." She turned toward me and paced the floor, like an attorney presenting a closing argument to a jury. She pounded the brush up and down in her hand like a noiseless gavel.

"Hank really didn't like my job because of all the weird hours. He was always complaining that I was never home. I guess in the last few months I haven't been. Rick and I would just go out for a bite and wind up talking for hours.

"Then I'd go home and Hank would be asleep on his books. I used to get mad when I saw that. It was like I was rationalizing that the whole fling with Rick was all right because Hank was so busy with his books he didn't have time for my needs. A few days ago I found out that he fell asleep on his books because he was waiting up for me—he'd been worried. He was just worried about the wrong thing. It wasn't my safety but my heart that he should have been concerned about."

Why So Many Affairs?

The generation affected by the sexual revolution bought into the "if it feels good—do it" mentality. They get restless if their personal needs are going unmet. Professional and personal schedules can lead to isolation and loneliness as the rising technology of our society keeps every waking minute busy. Lonely people go in search of a heart to be connected to and a body to touch.

Jeff Greenfield, commenting on the baby boomers, says, "For boomers, experience has moved at a breathless pace: TV instead of books; sex now, not after marriage; sensation now, at the flick of the remote control; marital problems solved with a quickie divorce."[1]

One survey of men explored the reasons for extramarital affairs. An overwhelming 78 percent listed physical and emotional attraction, while only 41 percent cited marital dissatisfaction. It seems some men who say they are satisfied with their marital partner still look for a thrill outside their own bedroom walls. The same report listed the occurrence of men cheating on their wives at 23 percent.[2] But men can't seem to make up their minds. When asked whom they liked more, their lover or their wife, men chose their wives.[3]

The controversial *Hite Report on Male Sexuality* listed the occurrence as much higher, with nearly three-fourths of the married men claiming they had had sex with someone other than their wives.[4]

One author noted a common thread in women who have had affairs: "They feel entitled to their love affairs."[5] A woman may feel vulnerable when her sexual libido rises in her thirties. Her marriage may seem cold or boring or her personal responsibilities overwhelming, so she longs for an escape.[6]

Helen Gurley Brown, editor of *Cosmopolitan* magazine, said on a recent talk show, "I don't think you have to have a raging affair with somebody's husband. I'm just saying: Use him, he can do something for you. And it's okay."[7]

However, in this desperate search for thrill and happiness, men and women forget or ignore the long-term consequences that are neither thrilling nor happy. Having an affair, or even toying with allowing emotional dependence on someone other than your spouse, can crush your marital sex life.

Does More Commitment Equal Better Sex?

"Recent evidence indicates that trust may be one of the most important factors determining orgasmic capacity in women," notes Helen Sanger Kaplan.[8] This is because women need to totally let go to experience orgasm. If a wife can't depend on her partner outside the bedroom, chances are she won't trust him inside either.

In a study of 500 women, the most common sexual problem

cited was the inability to experience orgasm. "Overall, there was enough evidence to suggest that a woman's ability to reach orgasm is tied to her feelings about loss. Apparently, the more she feels she cannot depend on being able to hold onto the people she values, the more limited she is in her orgasmic capacity."[9]

It is very difficult for a woman to become fully aroused when in her head loom thoughts like, *Is he comparing me to last night's tryst?* or *I'm so afraid he won't be here tomorrow.* It can be as subtle as *He slept with other women before our marriage. Does he miss it? Am I good enough to keep him interested? He's talked a lot about Janie from the office. They even had lunch together yesterday. I wonder if . . .*

"If" is all it takes in a woman's mind to keep her from experiencing a fully orgasmic encounter. And if she is holding back in her response during sex, most likely she is holding back in her assertiveness and spontaneity toward her husband as well. Therefore, husbands are doing themselves a favor when they establish a pattern of trustworthiness and concrete commitment.

In fact, overall, three-fifths of men and women say sex is better after marriage.[10] A clear pattern is seen: *The deeper the commitment, the deeper the level of intimacy and arousal.*

Why Risk a Great Sex Life?

In the same way, a husband can be harmed by a wife who has other lovers. Even the hint of comparison can push a husband into a performance spiral down the road to impotence. One doctor describes this downward spin in this way:

> He is pressured by the fear of failure. He concentrates on his bodily reactions like a spectator at his own lovemaking until self-consciousness destroys all joy and abandonment and sensation of pleasure. He tries, without success, to command sexual reflexes, but they respond only to desire and stimulation. He becomes like a person "who can't do anything right."[11]

In one survey, one-third of men and one-fourth of women say they have had an affair, even though 83 percent say affairs seriously affect the marriage.[12] Affairs actually are irrational when the consequences are added up. There seems to be a schizophrenia when it comes to sex and marriage.

Affairs are dangerous! *Affairs lower individual sexual satisfaction in the long run and place the stability of the marriage in danger.* Divorce then becomes an alternative that puts children, finances and sometimes careers in jeopardy. This is an awful lot to risk, so what is the rationale? Following are some of the reasons this "if it feels good, anything goes," hormone-driven generation gives:

1. Affairs are only natural.

This generation *expects* affairs to occur. At least 35 percent of Generation X says it is impossible to have a successful marriage and 61 percent expect most adults will divorce in the first five years of marriage.[13] Of this group, 20 percent has had sex with a married person.[14] Almost a third of this group also feels it is nearly impossible to have a friendship with a member of the opposite sex unless intercourse is involved.[15]

Men are especially vulnerable to affairs. They are twice as likely to have an affair and seem to be less willing to end the affair when there is still hope of saving their marriage.[16] Two-thirds of the men who have an affair will repeat this pattern and cheat again. Forty percent of women are repeat offenders.[17]

Monogamy is defined in the dictionary as one sexual partner for a *lifetime.* Yet a recent study defined monogamy as "having no more than one sexual partner in the past year."[18]

After the film *Indecent Proposal* came out, Oprah Winfrey surveyed people for her show. She asked, "Would you allow your wife to sleep with a stranger for $1 million?" Surprisingly, 55 percent said yes.[19]

The societal walls of protection around marriage have been

knocked down. Therefore, it is now up to married individuals to fortify themselves against the expectation that one or both will have an affair, or several, during their life together.

2. It's easier.

In our society, a divorce is easily obtained. The legal convenience of escaping a relationship lulls people into thinking divorce will be emotionally convenient too.

"Rick was there for me; my husband wasn't," Tiffany explained. "I felt second place with Hank, but when I was with Rick, I felt like a princess. But just recently, Hank made time for me and set up a nice romantic weekend for us. I felt so guilty. Hank finally opened up and started talking. He had been screaming so loudly about my hours because he missed me. He felt second place in my life.

"I can't believe we could live in the same house and get our wires so crossed!" Tiffany lamented. "Sometimes I shudder at how easy it was to almost lose it all with Hank—just because we weren't talking! Rick was fun, but he is married too! The whole thing was way too complicated. Rick was just too convenient!"

Daniel Pearlman and Steve Duck, authors of *Intimate Relationships*, note, "People exit when they have little to lose by doing so and believe that what they've got is not worth saving." People leave a marriage, "*when they have invested little in their relationships*, and when they are faced with what they regard as serious relationship problems."[20]

3. The cost seems small.

From the outside, extramarital sex seems alluring and inviting to many people. Hollywood exaggerates the thrills of new romance and forbidden love. Sex outside marriage is the sultry scene. Sex inside marriage is rarely shown, and when it is, it's tepid rather than steamy.

Noted movie critic Michael Medved asks, "Did you ever notice how few movies there are about happily married people? There are very few movies about married people at all, but those that are made tend to portray marriage as a disaster, as a dangerous battleground."[21]

Hollywood and the media, however, usually cloak the repugnant ramifications of an affair. Occasionally, they play them up, as in the movie *Fatal Attraction,* in which Michael Douglas has an affair with Glenn Close. He subsequently rejects her and she comes after him with a knife.

Short of being murdered for your indiscretion, let's consider some of the other consequences. There are many, if one is honest.

Logically, we know there is the horrible risk of AIDS and other sexually transmitted diseases. Sandra, a woman whose husband had a brief affair, shared these thoughts, "I want to forgive Tyler. But it was just so hard finding out from my gynecologist that I have a disease because my husband had an affair. I knew something was wrong with me and I suspected something was wrong in our marriage; now I have added agony—the treatment for these warts. I'm angry. Tyler feels guilty twice over, once for my emotional pain and once for my physical pain."

Sandra continued, "He says it's over. It'll never happen again. But how can I trust him anymore? I know he needs me to desire him physically again, but the logistics of intercourse are painful. When I start to reach out to him in that way, I see her with him and I want to slug him in the stomach instead!"

Sometimes the emotional harm becomes a series of broken relationships. The following unsigned letter, published by the *Grand Rapids Press,* expresses the pain and heartache of a broken home: "I'm going through a divorce, and it is no picnic. I have two children that I don't see often enough. I'm alone most of the time, and time is all I have. If you are married, live it up—but live it up with your spouse and not someone else's. The heartbreak of losing years of your life, your wife and your children nearly kills you. It is as if you have died." This man concluded his letter by saying, "I hope you never have the hurt I have had."[22]

At other times the children pay the piper for their parents' mistakes. One brother explained it this way, "Dad had blatant affairs, and the worst part of it was that he tried to make the women a part of the family. One woman . . . he brought home to dinner a lot. Dad was obviously sexually involved with her. He'd flirt with her outrageously. The fact that he tried to make us one big happy family and be friends was what was so disgusting.

"It affected my sister in a very bad way. She became very sexual, and my parents, although they tried to control her at first, absolutely couldn't. She hung out with a street gang and had sex with almost all of them. She wouldn't ever use the term love. She talks about sex all the time, but much too graphic for my taste. Dad would just laugh in an embarrassed sort of way and change the subject."[23]

Hidden Costs to Personal Sexuality

Finally, the consequence that is most hidden is the change that takes place in a person's own heart and mind when an affair is consummated.

"I'm not sure I trust myself anymore," said Tiffany. "I used to rely on my feelings and instincts, but I feel they let me down. I thought I was in love with Rick, but now I think it was a sort of infatuation.

"It was an unreal world Rick and I lived in. I never had to discuss the mortgage with him, or car problems, or who was going to pick up the dry cleaning.

"Hank and I had the real issues to deal with day in and day out. But that got to be all we talked about. And I still had all these other feelings that weren't being expressed—so I guess I went looking for a sympathetic listening ear.

"The problem was, when Rick and I began planning stuff other than the next time we would be together, we started fighting too. Now my feelings are all confused. I'm not even sure if I know the difference between love and lust."

Counselor Stephen Arterburn explains the difference between love and lust in this way:

Love is personal; lust is impersonal. Love is concrete, focused on a particular object; lust is unfocused, capable of fixing on almost any available object. Love tends toward faithfulness; lust is a wanderer. Love seeks stability; lust is short-lived and mercurial. Love is an affair of the mind and heart; lust is an affair of the emotions and hormones. Love is a matter of giving; lust is a matter of taking.[24]

Add to these confused feelings a wife's depleted ability to experience orgasm because she mistrusts her husband, or a man's impotence because of performance anxiety, and you have a short-circuited sexual relationship. Just jumping ship and beginning a new relationship doesn't solve the problem. The woman will carry into the new relationship a lack of trust in men and the man will carry the fear of performing well.

How Can We Recover?

We (Jim and Sally) have written a book to deal with the overwhelming effects of an affair, or the threat of an affair, in a marriage. *When a Mate Wants Out* details the road back to wholeness as a person and as a couple. It is a work that must be done slowly and thoroughly, but *rebuilding is possible.*[25]

Our ministry, Mid-Life Dimensions, focuses primarily on helping couples save their marriages. We receive thousands of letters telling of fear, despair and confusion as a marriage starts to fall apart. But it is exciting to us to see about half of the couples we work with resolve their serious problems, even an affair, and experience a restored marriage. There is hope!

Building Couple Confidence

The first and most important key is to reestablish the desire for commitment. This same step is applicable if you and your partner were sexually active before marriage, have had an affair during marriage or are simply tossing out phrases that would undermine confidence.

For example, in times of anger, couples will say things such as, "Well, if you don't appreciate me, I know someone who does." Or, "Maybe I won't come home tonight." Sometimes couples will remind their spouse of all the fun they had in past relationships. Couples in these patterns need to remove others from their private party. They need to get rid of memories and remarks about others and reestablish their vow of "cling only unto you."

Tiffany called me the following year. She wanted to get together. She said she had some exciting news to share over lunch.

"We redid our vows!" exclaimed Tiffany. "It felt so good to come clean with Hank. We got counseling. I'm learning to trust my husband to meet my emotional needs and he's learning to trust my commitment to him. It's hard work but it is paying off!

"The pastor who counseled us told us about one man he knew who had an affair and when their marriage got restored, they renewed their wedding vows. They had their teenage kids as the bridesmaids and groomsmen. He gave his wife a new ring and he gave each of his children rings too. He wanted them to have a visible symbol of his renewed promise, especially since he saw the bad effects of his affair on all their lives. Even though we don't have kids yet, I still wanted to reaffirm my love to Hank. The ceremony did that. The scar will always be there but the wounds are hurting less every day."

Maybe you or your spouse has been unfaithful. Or perhaps you are playing with adulterous thoughts in your head or making remarks that are undercutting the confidence in your marriage. Maybe you have an emotional dependence on someone other than your spouse and your own feelings are beginning to scare you.

There is hope. A step to reaffirm your commitment toward your spouse will go a long way, even if he or she doesn't reciprocate immediately. You have opened the door of your heart to allow deeper intimacy to develop in the future. By verbalizing your commitment to faithfulness, you can build a bridge to your mate's heart, which will become an open channel for pleasure and passion.

Pleasure Point:

Choose a trust exchange: a symbol of your commitment to fidelity from now on. Or make the gift symbolize a thank-you for your mate's remaining faithful. In a private ceremony, exchange the gifts, sharing verbally and in writing your feelings about what the gift symbolizes.

7

THE
PLEASURE OF
AUTHENTIC
DESIRE

SHEILA'S HEART POUNDED WITH passion. The beat of calypso music rushed through her veins as she read:

"Oh, Rebecca," Alex said as he pulled her body next to his. She could feel every heartbeat as it pulsed wildly in his chest. Alex cradled her head of flowing black tresses as his hand caressed her thighs.

"You are the most beautiful woman on the island and I have ached to hold you in my arms since the day I first saw you step off the boat. Your dark eyes contained a mystery I had to solve. I must know your secrets," Alex panted as he engulfed her in his muscular arms. His head was now buried between her breasts and his wind-tossed hair felt soft and playful as it rested beneath her chin. She could feel his warm, moist lips dancing down the neckline of her sundress. Rebecca ran her fingers up the back of her tanned, throbbing lover. She longed for him to know her, to know all of her. Alex ripped at the shoulder of her dress—

Suddenly the mystery of the sexual spell was broken.

"Hi, Hon. What's for dinner?" Jerry bellowed cheerfully. She looked up at her husband. He was thirty pounds overweight, had a plastic pocket protector in his rumpled dress shirt and smelled like the inside of his factory.

She was livid. *Eat!* she thought. *He doesn't need to eat! Look at him. A dictionary definition of couch potato. Boredom incarnate. He wouldn't know romance if it hit him over the head.* She didn't even bother to get up. "There are leftovers in the fridge," she mumbled.

Jerry walked into the kitchen. He considered kissing his wife on the way. *But what's the use?* he thought.

Sheila turned on the nightly soaps, popped open her book, and wandered in her dream world long after Jerry had gone to bed. When she crawled in next to him, he reached over for her and she simply remarked, "Not tonight." She closed her eyes, hoping "Alex" would meet her as she slept.

Addicted to Fantasy

Barbara DeAngelis says, "No one deliberately sets out to destroy his or her own sex life. But many of us have some bad sexual habits that inhibit passion." She goes on to explain that often people spend time contemplating what should have happened rather than enjoying what is happening. They become spectators to their own love life.[1]

Secondhand lovemaking can take many forms. It can be a constant stream of romance novels, sultry TV shows or lusty movies, or the compulsive buying of the newest in lingerie and perfume. Addiction can be anything, from urging friends to unleash morsels about their own sex lives to taping every sexy talk show for the vicarious thrill of others' exploits.

Grant Martin, author of *When Good Things Become an Addiction,* notes, "Romance addicts can get high from a daydream, a song, a scene, a romantic memory or a cause. Everywhere the addict turns in our society, there is a source for the fix. Media, movies, TV and advertisements can all be sources for a mood-altering experience. The problem, as with any addiction, is that the fix is never enough."[2]

Science has discovered that the process of falling in love actually produces a substance called PEA that is like an endorphin. When released, it leads to feelings of excitation, exhilaration and euphoria. Some people get hooked on the feeling of love rather than nurturing the connection to the lover.[3] Those who are in love with love will spend more and more time finding ways to create this high. They will isolate themselves from their spouse, family, work and friends. Some try riskier behavior that can lead to unwanted affairs, dangerous conduct or illegal endeavors.

Martin has charted four levels of romantic addiction:

Level one is primarily fantasy. An example would be a mother who cannot attend her child's event because her favorite soap is on. Another example is the woman who is so engrossed in a novel that the needs of her family go unnoticed and unmet. Affairs are justified in this phase because the addict sees the spouse as unable to meet romantic expectations.

Level two leads to the acting out of fantasies. Affairs, romantic encounters and multiple marriages can all be ways of acting out fantasies. The addict has a difficult time controlling behavior and becomes increasingly insensitive to his or her spouse. Family, sense of right and wrong, and personal integrity all begin to decline.

Level three finds the addict in a desperate search for a romantic high. The person may spend large sums of money, may even get involved with strangers or travel to faraway places. The desperate romantic may seek out danger just for a thrill. Cultural values are ignored, families are destroyed and violence may be acted out to get the thrill.

Level four is compulsively violent behavior. The addict becomes unable to get a romantic high unless danger or violence is present. Romantic addicts at this point may seek out the thrill of being with an emotionally troubled or potentially dangerous person. They make no pretense about having a relationship. It is just the thrill of unsailed romantic seas that compels them.[4]

"I just want to fall in love again," said Sheila a year after our first conversation. "Jerry only wants to stay home. I've been going out with my girlfriend, Laura, and her husband, Trent. We go dancing and to parties. Lots of single guys are there and they treat me nice. Jerry hates it. He's jealous. He's sure I'm going to have an affair! If he really wants me, why doesn't he take me dancing? Why can't Jerry be fun like Trent or the other guys at the club?"

The Silent Killer
Comparison can be a hidden danger to intimacy if friends compare notes. Studies are frequently released that detail exploits of married couples across the nation. These seem to say everyone should meet the standard, and that makes it difficult to maintain individuality as a couple. Actually, it's okay that each couple is uniquely different in their methods and frequency of sex. No couple should be a copy of anyone else.

One author notes that "there are times when almost any advice can seize one with feelings of inadequacy. It's normal for a couple not to make love every night."[5] Illness, job schedules and children's needs are common roadblocks that hinder sexual intimacy. Sometimes the act of intercourse will be impossible, but emotional and physical closeness can still be maintained. Intimacy apart from sex will cultivate a bed for passion to flourish in the future.

I (Pam) have to be careful not to compare Bill now with Bill the first five to seven years of our marriage. Bill is currently carrying a mountain of responsibility so the frequency of his romantic gestures has lessened. He is still very romantic and attentive, but when I compare him to his former self, he can't compete. Bill learned the hard way how to let himself off the hook and lower his own expectations of himself.

We started a pattern during our early years of marriage of setting aside a day to spoil one another for a birthday present. About six years into our marriage, my birthday fell in the middle of Bill's grad school deadlines, the demands of his ministry as a youth pastor and a drafting job he had taken on.

Knowing that he hadn't been as attentive during the semester as he knew I'd like him to be, he then crammed into one four-hour slot what usually would have taken us a day and a half to enjoy. He was out to conquer my birthday just like his other deadlines. He rushed me from place to place, constantly checking his watch. After he reeled off the next several "fun" things on the agenda, I said, "Really, Bill. It's okay. We don't have to do it all just because it's my birthday. Is it okay if we just slow down and enjoy where we are? Just being with you is the best present I could receive from you." A look of relief came over his face.

Even your stresses are unique to you as a couple. They can either be building blocks for intimacy or bricks in a wall that separates you from each other. When multiple problems attack you, hug each other and talk, rather than comparing yourselves with the intimacy of another couple or with your past memories.

In one study, couples who rated their marital happiness as *high* experienced no greater frequency in sexual intercourse than the average couple.[6] "Sex isn't everything to happily married couples," says physician Mary Ann Bartusis.[7]

When couples have sex at their own pace, it's actually better. They can choose the best times and places so that sex itself doesn't become boring but remains fun.

Couples therapist David Treadway agrees: "The idea is to escape the tyranny of 2.2 sexual episodes a week, to find your own secret garden."[8]

Unique Is What You Seek

"It's hard for me," Sheila told me (Sally) one night. "Most of my friends have very sensitive, caring husbands—but Jerry just isn't like that. I know I can't expect him to be who he isn't, but sometimes it's hard not to compare him with other men."

Sheila has been caught in a vicious cycle where neither she nor Jerry can find fulfillment. If she continually places Jerry next to all the men in the world, Jerry will continue to come up short. No man is an Adonis. Perfect men are found only in Greek myths and other legends. The ideal is always perfect, but the real man can never match the ideal. And the ideal man isn't in Sheila's bed each night.

If Sheila continues to grade Jerry based on other people's experiences, rather than accepting and appreciating him as he is, Jerry will never be free to respond to her. Instead of being motivated to change, he will quit trying or look somewhere else.

The media, conversations with friends and even scientific studies can raise unrealistic expectations about our marital relationships. Comparison substitutes a pasteboard ideal for a real, live partner and robs the marriage of its uniqueness and identity. As the ideal is elevated and dwelled on, the real partner diminishes in size. Remember, it is the living, breathing husband or wife who really has the ability to meet needs, to fulfill hopes and dreams.

Every romantic notion should be evaluated through a grid which asks, "Can I share this with my spouse, giving him or her the opportunity to participate?" If your mate chooses not to fulfill your wish, ask yourself, "Can I love and appreciate my spouse for that decision? Can I let the fantasy die and appreciate my spouse for who he or she is?"

In a study on men's needs, admiration was high on the list.[9] As a man is appreciated for his unique ability to please his wife, he will repeat the words or action so that he will be "rewarded" again with praise. As the husband learns to repeat things the wife appreciates and the wife learns to easily express more admiration to her thoughtful husband, a healthy pattern is established. Rather than belittling a male for his lack of romance, a woman should acknowledge it when her husband does use his unique ability to treat her as special.

The wife of an unexpressive husband may have to look hard for the special kindnesses he is trying to extend. He may think it is romantic of him to change the oil in the car and keep his wife on reliable wheels. How about being a brave woman by sliding under the car and whispering your appreciation to him as he works? Seek to speak the same "language of love" as your spouse. You'll find excellent insights in the little book *How Do You Say, "I Love You"?* by Judson Swihart, which describes eight languages of love and how you can use them.

Conversely, in the same survey, women said they longed for affection, conversation, honesty and openness. The savvy lover will want to create times when his wife can receive an extra little touch, a special caress, a passing pat and, most of all, a listening ear. Men and women crave the words "You are a great lover." The best way to free your lover to excel in intimacy is to release him or her from the trap of comparison.

Real Live Fun

Remember Sheila? Well, she was starting to change her approach to Jerry and to those steamy novels.

"I started thanking Jerry for the little things," said Sheila. "You know, his playing ball with the kids, his fixing dinner on a hectic day and keeping the yard looking nice. I tried to let him know how little things added to my feelings of romance toward him. After he finished working in the yard, I took him some lemonade. As he was standing there all smelly and sweaty, I told him how the yard reminded me of a forest glen and how I'd always dreamed of making love in the forest. I thought he was going to choke on the lemonade, but then his eyes lit up! I had thought long and hard about whether I should say it because I might have to follow through with it. I had been living in a dream world— now it was time for real live fun."

Sabotage of Sex Therapy

Another avenue that may destroy your sex life with unrealistic expectations is randomly collecting sex therapy and how-to books and videos. Sexual advice is plentiful, but couple-building material is like finding a needle in a haystack. Sexology became a growing industry in the 1960s. The industry has had such growth potential that many companies market money-producing commodities as if they were sound sex therapy tools.[10]

Sexual clinics and therapy groups sprang up overnight. At the Institute for Advanced Study of Human Sexuality, nudity was en-couraged, as well as erotic massage and self-stimulation. Many therapies were conducted in the hot tub. In one class, students were to stand naked in front of a mirror and talk about their bodies with the class. It was explained that "No rules prohibit sexual interaction among participants as long as they do not have sex in the building."[11]

Unfortunately, perverted sex therapists have tainted the repu-tation of all sex therapists. Some sexologists routinely have sex with their clients or carry on other damaging practices.[12] The drawback to much of modern sex therapy is that an intimate circle of two becomes an ever-broadening commune.

Even well-intentioned sex therapists can erode the specialness that belongs in the intimate couple's sexual expression by making it commonplace and clinical. Proper sexual advice strives to keep the relationship private.

Healthy writings and consultations have a goal of sequestering as much of the couple's sexuality as possible while giving necessary and vital knowledge needed to solve problems. Cloistering love to only the couple is to protect a precious commodity from exploitation. We are not condemning sex therapists; there may be times when a couple needs such a therapist. But a therapist should promote "coupleness," not subtly drive you apart.

One very excellent resource of good sexual advice is Ed Wheat, a medical doctor who has written several books on marital sex. He describes this marital privacy as "a walled garden, the inner courtyard . . . sacred place . . . a private little kingdom . . . removed from public view, secluded, not for common use."[13]

Even the word *intimacy* is a derivative of the Latin "intimus" which means "inner or innermost."[14] Sharing of needs, openness and vulnerability are the common threads of true intimacy.

One therapist says it is only with time that true passion is built—because it takes time to build trust. "You have to be willing to get to know yourself and your partner intimately—and let him get to know you."[15]

Sexual advice and input should always maintain the oneness of the marital relationship. That has been our goal in this book. We want to shed insight while maintaining your privacy and ours.

Romance addiction produces an idealistic, unreal lover. Comparison brings unrealistic expectations. Sex therapies sometimes bring unrealistic intrusions into your unique sexual relationship.

Protecting Your Oneness

Unity between you and your spouse is a precious treasure. To protect that intimacy, a couple needs to evict all the real and imaginary lovers from the marriage. To do so, take a break from external stimulation, such as videos, magazines, how-to books, novels, soap operas, even advice from friends. During this time, each partner should evaluate how such stimulation is affecting your relationship.

You may feel as if your spouse is expecting you to be someone you aren't, or you may be dreaming of your spouse riding in on a white horse and fulfilling your wildest dreams. Both daydreams polarize you and your love by chaining you to the unreal.

To have great sex and a good marriage, the unreal must be shunned and the illusions shed, while the genuine and authentic is embraced.

Often, after an especially satisfying sexual and intimate time with Bill, I (Pam) slip out of bed and pen poems or snatches of remembrances. I then leave them as a thank-you on Bill's mirror or pillow. I write words for our eyes only—it's our personal novel. Our love isn't fictional. Our love is as real as the words on this page.

Instead of pretending to be characters in a steamy novel, God can help you write your own love story. A story to be lived out on the pages of your life with each other.

Pleasure Point:

Take your spouse off the treadmill of unrealistic expectations by making a list of character traits or romantic gestures he or she has already brought to your marriage. Buy a beautiful thank-you card and list the things for which you are thankful. Mail it to your spouse's place of work or leave it on a pillow or in another romantic spot.

Then sort through any sources of sexual comparison (books, magazines, videos). Decide which encourage a hedge of privacy around you and your mate. Get rid of the rest.

Three key questions that may help you decide are:

1. Am I addicted to anything in these materials?

2. Does the advice in these materials help me to unconditionally love my mate with full acceptance of who he or she is? Or am I using this information unfairly as a measuring rod for my mate?

3. Does the advice in these materials make our love life less private?

8

THE
PLEASURE
OF
SELF-CONTROL

J AMES BRYDEN WRITES, "LOVE DOES not die easily. It is a living thing. It thrives in the face of all life's hazards, save one—neglect."[1]

Brian was in his early twenties when he came to my (Bill's) office to talk alone. He was angry because I had told his wife, Kaye, that pornography should not be a part of their sexual experience with one another. Brian has always been an independent thinker and did not like getting such bold advice from someone he didn't know very well.

Brian was obviously uncomfortable, but he was intent on winning me over to his point of view. After very little small talk he blurted out, "So what's the big deal with looking at pictures of naked women? Didn't God create the human body? And isn't the body beautiful?"

"Yes, God did create the human body," I replied, trying to disarm Brian's assumptions. "And yes, the human body is beautiful. But Brian, do you need to use pornography in order to love your wife?"

Brian was apparently stunned by the directness of this question as he began thinking out loud, "No, my wife and I have a good sex life and we would have a good sex life whether we watched X-rated movies or not."

"Does your wife want to watch pornography?" I continued.

"No," Brian said hesitantly.

"Most women say that pornography makes them feel used," I responded. "And men who are honest with themselves say that pornography controls them. A marriage cannot last a lifetime when you feel manipulated and your wife feels exploited."

"Come on, Bill, how can you think that lifelong marriage works anymore? Do you honestly believe that a man can be satisfied with only one woman? You can't really expect that! It would be so boring!"

"Well, it doesn't have to be." I responded. "My wife and I have a very satisfying relationship and our sex life continues to get better."

"Yeah, but you've never done the things I've done. You haven't seen the things I've seen. You live a very sheltered life so it doesn't take much to give you a thrill!"

Brian sat thinking to himself. I could almost read his mind. How could this man truly believe that sex with only one woman could be as good as all the sexual experiences he had had? How could I expect him to change?

Brian tried to explain away the nagging dissatisfaction of his own life as he told the story of his quest for the sexual fulfillment he believed was his right. He bragged about the women he had "conquered" as a young man. He touted his venture into soft pornography, then hard pornography, and justified his daily addiction to pornographic material by pointing out that all "real" men did the same.

"Do you think I am a real man?" I asked him.

"Well, yes, I think you are a godly man and I respect you." Brian didn't want to offend his pastor but he really didn't think that a religious man understood sex. He hoped I would drop this line of questioning.

"I don't look at pornography. By your definition I am not a real man," I continued, much to Brian's discomfort.

Brian's half-hearted retaliation exposed the vulnerability he was beginning to feel, "You are not supposed to look at pornography. You're a pastor!"

"Am I not a man because I am a pastor?"

At this point Brian realized he was trying to cover up his own pain by discrediting his pastor. The dam of his pent-up emotions broke loose as he told of the haunting pictures in his head, from childhood years, of his father, mother and other women engaging in sexual activity. Brian took time to listen to himself for the first time in his life.

"Why does my dad have to be a pervert? Why did I have to get a dad who would do those things to my mom? Why did my mom let those things happen? What's wrong with me that I have to have these parents?"

Brian's flood of emotions laid bare the source of his personal involvement in the sexual revolution. He did not respect his dad because his dad had abused his mom. He did not respect his mom because she had allowed herself to be abused.

His response was to abuse his own sexuality so that he fit into the family. It was too painful to say his mom and dad were wrong.

In utter frustration he told me that he didn't know how to relate to women without being sexually involved. He avoided all contact with women that wouldn't lead to sex.

In one final explosion of pain and frustration, Brian exclaimed, "After all I have experienced, I don't think I can look at the woman I married with respect—as if she is a real person. I'm afraid I will only look at her as a sex object. But, do you really think I can change?"

Trying to Fill the Void

For children of the sexual revolution who want to have a lasting marriage relationship, the pornography issue is explosive. This generation has been bombarded with graphic sexual entertainment and flooded with opportunities to indulge every sexual imagination. Many boast of their newfound freedom and brag about their guilt-free lifestyle.

Tragically, though, a rising number in the post-sexual-revolution generation have found that being thrust into sexual experiments outside of marriage has threatened their ability to build a lasting marriage relationship.

The pornography issue became a crisis for Brian when he met Kaye. He honestly loved Kaye but was afraid he would be too sexually restless to build a lasting marriage. Despite his fears, Brian and Kaye got married. For the first few months, Brian thought his struggle was over as he and Kaye seemed to be sexually compatible.

In time though, the thrill began to deteriorate as the allure of new experiences demanded Brian's attention. To fill the void, Brian started bringing home movies that depicted couples engaging in various sexual activities. He convinced his wife to watch these movies with him and then try to perform the acts they viewed.

For Brian the excitement returned. He felt like new life had been breathed into their sex life. He couldn't understand why Kaye had grown colder toward him.

Kaye didn't understand why Brian needed these movies. "Am I not exciting enough for you?" she asked.

She wished Brian would love her just for herself, rather than for her body. But she was afraid she'd lose him if she refused to participate. She really loved Brian, but she was repulsed by the things he asked her to do.

The Empty Well for Men

This struggle for Brian and Kaye existed because pornography is an empty well. The well is empty for men because it can never satisfy. Men are easily aroused by visual images; that makes them targets of pornography. Initially, the graphic nature of pornography attracts the aggressive nature of men and makes them think that a need is being met.

In an environment of constant sexual stimulation, this aggressive nature cries out for more graphic displays and can even turn to a darker side—sexual violence. The more frequently a man watches pornography, the more graphic and violent the pornography must become to produce the same level of arousal.[2]

Brian, like most men, didn't think he would become violent, but if he continued to depend on pornography to help bring excitement to his marriage relationship, he was guaranteeing his own dissatisfaction. At first, it would seem as if the entertainment was working. But if he continued, he would find the level of absurdity and violence had to increase to reach the previous level of sexual pleasure.

The Feeling's Gone

We have observed that depression is associated with prolonged exposure to pornography. Depression affects all aspects of life, including sexuality. Research has discovered that "compared to healthy men, depressed men reported less frequent sexual thoughts and fantasies, less frequent sexual activity, less pleasure from their sexual activity, and less satisfaction with their sex lives."[3]

One man, addicted to pornography for ten years, grieved over its effects on his life. His angst came to a turning point after seeking out a peep show where quarters allowed him to gaze at women rotating around on a platter while they masturbated. He thought: "There is no art, no beauty, no acrobatic dancing. The woman is obviously a sex object and nothing else. The men are isolated, caged voyeurs. There is no relationship."[4]

Days later he took a trip down the coast, filled with natural beauty, eating at his favorite restaurants, and lodging at his favorite bed and breakfasts. As he stopped to gaze over the windswept ocean, he mused about the numbness that had taken residence in his heart: "I felt no pleasure. None. My emotional reaction was the same as if I'd been at home, yawning, reading the newspaper. All romance had been drained out, desiccated. . . . Was I going crazy? Would I lose every worthwhile sensation in life? Was my soul leaking away?"[5]

The Silent Agony for Women

The well is also empty for women, because the acts depicted in pornography are stressful to women. One woman, after years of silent agony, was finally willing to admit her husband was addicted to pornography; she gave the following testimony before the Attorney General's Commission on Pornography:

> He made me want to die—every time he took me to bed—and I felt he wanted to destroy who I am. His triumph over me was controlling me in bed and making me feel what he felt. He didn't love me—there was no feeling of comfort or fulfillment, only pain, emptiness and deep loneliness.[6]

As a couple participates in pornographic activities, their relationship inevitably suffers. The woman feels used and the man is left with the frustrating reality that he is the only one pleased with the performance. Loneliness and alienation set in and the couple finally concludes they cannot meet one another's needs.

The Downward Spiral

Even hard-core pornography users are admitting that a spiral of alienation occurs when pornography is introduced as a partner in a relationship. One young man, who had been involved in sadomasochism and the pornography business, got married, then had children. He says he sees nothing wrong in his addiction to erotica or in sharing some of it with his children, but his comments reveal the inherent numbing effect it has.

"I don't think my kids are ready for it. Hard-core becomes very detached. . . . I guess it's the impersonalness of the tape that I'm not sure they can deal with."[7]

Although he is not willing to face it for himself, he does recognize that pornography makes a very personal expression of love impersonal. This alienation spins downward through unmet expectations, which leads to withdrawal from real sex into fantasy and masturbation. Finally the spiral leads to anger, because neither the real-life sex partner nor his own body can keep pace with his erotic fantasies.

The Road to Sexual Fulfillment

The road to fulfillment is found in a whole new well to drink from. Sex is a very special gift that has been given to married couples to enhance their adventure through life. The adventure involves a curious exploration of the multiple possibilities a couple can discover to express their sexual love for each another.

As the couple continues to grow with one another, the intimacy builds. New possibilities for romantic and sexual expression are naturally found. But lifelong sexual innovation is possible only if the couple values the relationship and continues to grow. When pornography is used, the exploration process is accelerated so that the couple engages in physical activity beyond their own personal comfort level.

The natural discovery process is assassinated by the demands on the couple to perform up to the level of the entertainment. If an intimate relationship is reduced to a performance, the inevitable result is frustration and insecurity. Sexual success in any marriage requires that the discovery of sexual fulfillment happen at the pace comfortable to the couple, not that dictated by pornography.

The Key to Sexual Success

The key to sexual success is balance. The couple should be open to the process of discovery that is inherent in any intimate relationship. When new approaches to the couple's lovemaking are uncovered, they both must remain open to the possibilities.

A wife should have the courage to listen to her husband's needs and pleasure choices, but she must not allow herself to be reduced to a performer on the stage of her husband's self-seeking fantasies. It is okay to say no in the midst of an intimate relationship when a woman feels that she is being taken advantage of rather than being loved.

Kaye had tried unsuccessfully many times to discuss her dissatisfaction with Brian's demands, so she was amazed when he approached her one day and wanted to talk about the coldness of their relationship.

"What is wrong with you, Kaye?" Brian asked with a bite in his words. "How come you never want to try the things I want to try?"

"I don't think anything is wrong with me. I am just a woman, and women don't like pornography," she responded, trying not to react defensively.

"Well, I know some women who like pornography," Brian added, "They think it's fun."

"I don't know those women, Brian. All the women I know are

threatened and turned off by watching others engage in sex. I just want to make love with you, and I want you to make love with me, not with the women on the TV."

Brian was listening, so Kaye went on. She spelled out in detail how she would like to be loved by him. Brian marveled as Kaye told Brian the romantic things he does that she appreciates. He felt close to her as she explained where and how she liked to be touched by him. He was pleased as she described how special she felt when he was spontaneous in their lovemaking. He felt ashamed as Kaye told him how ordinary and degraded she felt when she was repeating what they had watched on a pornographic movie.

This conversation opened up a new dimension in their relationship. Brian felt a renewed sense of pride in their marriage. Finally, he had figured out to how make Kaye feel special. He felt a new sense of courage in his intimate relationship with Kaye, as he came to understand her needs and desires. His sense of pride as a man was boosted as he saw he could arouse his wife, rather than focusing on only fulfilling his own desires.

Now, Kaye and he had a secret. They knew how to relate in a way that nobody else knew about. Understanding these mysteries about Kaye fired up a brand new desire in Brian. Eventually, Brian found enough security with Kaye to consider destroying the pornographic material he had diligently collected since puberty.

The Tough Choice

Brian was realizing that a man who wants to have a satisfying relationship with his wife must make the tough choice not to allow pornography to infiltrate his life and compete for his affection. He, like other men, discovered that authentic men don't need artificial devices to gain fulfillment. A billboard in Midland, Texas, that we (Jim and Sally) especially like pictures several men (noted sports and community leaders), with the caption

"REAL MEN DON'T NEED PORN."

A man must first learn to value his relationship with his wife above his own desires, if he wants to have a lifelong relationship that is sexually fulfilling. He must then decide to abstain from all pornographic material.

Remove the Strangler

The destructive effect of sexually graphic material on a man's life is illustrated by an example from nature:

In Mexico and the tropical zones of South America a so-called "strangler" fig grows in abundance. The fruit is not palatable except to cattle and birds. After the birds eat it, they must clean their beaks of the sticky residue. They do this by rubbing them on nearby trees. The seeds of the small fig have a natural glue which makes them adhere to the branches. When the rainy season arrives, germination takes place. Soon tiny roots make their way down into the heart of the wood and begin to grow. Within a few years the once lovely palms have become entirely covered with the entangling vines of the parasitic growth. Unless the "strangler" figs are removed, the tree will begin to wither, dropping one frond after another until it is completely lifeless. The only way to stop the killing process of the "strangler" fig is to take a sharp knife and cut away the invader.[8]

Developing a Plan of Action

In the same way, pornography will take root in the heart of any man and slowly steal his ability to love only one woman for a lifetime. If porn is a part of your life, the only way to put life back into your marriage is to take drastic measures and cut away the invader.

You must develop a plan of action toward sexually explicit material:

1. Decide to abstain from pornography.

2. Decide to focus only on ideas that promote your relationship with your wife.

3. Decide to avoid places that would tempt you to get involved in the downward spiral.

4. Meet regularly with two or three other men who are sympathetic to the problem and will provide compassionate accountability.

These men should be made familiar with your plan to avoid contact with pornography. They should be given permission to ask questions such as, "When was the last time you viewed pornography? Are you doing the things you said you would do to build your relationship with your wife? How close are you to falling back into pornography?"

Note: If pornography *addiction* has developed, special action should be pursued. We recommend talking with a trusted counselor. We have also included a list of recommended reading and counselors in appendix B at the end of the book for those who need to explore the subject further.

A Weekend of Freedom

Brian and Kaye are fortunate. Brian sensitively listened to his wife as she lovingly confronted him with her distaste for pornography. As a result of their courageous interaction, they decided their relationship was too valuable to threaten with pornography.

They planned a romantic weekend away at a hotel with one requirement—the room had to have a fireplace. They loaded the provocative collection of pornography in the trunk and headed off for their weekend of freedom.

After sharing a delightful dinner filled with candlelight and romantic conversation, they went to their room and built a warm fire. Seated on the hearth, they proceeded to place the articles of pornography in the fire.

While the material burned, a new sense of freedom came over

the couple. It was as if the unrealistic sexual demands they had placed on themselves were rising with the smoke and dissipating in the air. That night was one of the most memorable evenings of lovemaking Brian and Kaye have ever experienced, and the freedom introduced to their marriage has led to many more.

You may be feeling trapped by the escalation of explicit pictures you are carrying around in your head. You may be feeling discouraged or demoralized by the unreal performance expectations placed on you by a spouse entangled in the web of pornography. Hang in there. You can hack away the invading tentacles. You can take the bold step to say no to pornography and yes to each other.

Pleasure Point:

Gather all unrealistic expectation builders (pornography, explicit movies, novels and so on) and arrange for a bonfire. If a fireplace is not available, gather up all the material and shred it or smash it with a hammer so no one else will be exposed to it. Put is all in a trash bag and throw it out.

Then lay out a new white comforter or blanket as a symbol of wiping the slate clean, and enjoy your new sexual freedom together. Make love in front of the fire or at another special "new" location that says, "I release you from the 'fantasy sex syndrome' and I commit myself not to use pornography."

9

THE
PLEASURE
OF
PASSION

Allen, usually a stoic and composed business executive, was fighting back the tears as he sat across the lunch table from me (Bill). Choked with emotion, head in his hands, he poured out his panicked thoughts.

"It's like someone has thrown a bucket of cold water on me as I've awakened from a dream. Teresa is so important to me, but I haven't been treating her that way. I don't think she even likes to be with me anymore. Who could blame her?

"I treat her like one of the employees," Allen continued. "With all the financial stress at the company the past few years, and my time being so tight, I just expected her to pick up more slack at home. I told her not to expect anything from me. I just left lists of all I needed her to do.

"We decided she would be home with the kids while they were small, so we would be the ones raising them. In reality, she's been pretty much a single parent and I've treated her like my live-in maid, not my wife.

"It's no wonder when I reached out for her last night and told her I wanted her, she just said, 'Allen, it's been a long day. Okay?'

"That might have been okay, but I'm sure she winced when I touched her. It was like the thought of being with me was irritating or nauseating or something. I really love Teresa, but can I win her back?

"I tried buying her lots of nice things this week, but I overheard her tell her best friend, 'Yeah, Allen tried to buy my affections again. He just doesn't get it, does he?'

"No, I just *don't* get it!" he concluded, with frustration and fear in his voice.

The Key to Unleashing Sexual Passion

I explained to Allen that God cares about our love lives. In the Bible, God included an entire book that is a glimpse into the intimate life of one young couple. The husband was a powerful leader in his country, while his wife came from a rather modest upbringing. The husband, King Solomon, won the heart of his beloved bride with some very direct acts and words of kindness. And she also wooed and warmed her weary mate's heart with specific acts of kindness.

Kindness is like a beautifully painted backdrop that sets the stage for a romantic drama. In the Song of Solomon (also called the Song of Songs), both the husband and wife used kindness and understanding to evoke erotic love. This type of language not only gets an immediate response, but the residue of kindness remains to strengthen the marital bond.

The opposite is also true. Solomon in later years disregarded his own advice and broke this special bond when he took many wives for political gain. At the end of his life, he was cynical and disillusioned by his own promiscuity and said it was all vanity. He could have chosen to cultivate this beautiful monogamous relationship with a lifetime of sexual fulfillment, but he didn't.

Allen and I discussed how most of us believe we should use kindness and encouraging words with our mate. But neglect and selfishness cause us to quit finding the time, energy and creativity necessary to do the simplest acts or speak the words. By not watering and feeding this part of our relationship, we may find ourselves locked out of the garden of pleasure we once enjoyed.

What Is Passion?

Passion begins with an understanding of your mate. It means you know your spouse's insecurities, hopes, dreams and loves.

"I don't even know what Teresa likes anymore! It's as if we're strangers in the same house!" Allen said, as our conversation continued.

"Allen," I inquired, "have you tried asking her lately what she likes? What she's thinking about? What she'd like from you?"

"I tried," he said meekly.

"When she explained to you what she'd like, how did you respond?" I asked.

He said hesitantly, "Well, I guess I was a little defensive. I told her all the reasons why I couldn't do, or hadn't done what she wanted. That was a while ago. Now she won't talk about it."

"Allen," I said reassuringly, "try talking to her kindly. Praise her often and do small kind things for her for the next few days— then ask again."

I reminded Allen that verbal kindness and praise become an oasis for a marriage. Acts of kindness are springs that water our love and make our sex life blossom. Kind lovers are thoughtful lovers. They listen for the quiet comments which give insight into the heart. Then they respond gently in return.

Later that day, Teresa called me (Pam). "I just can't get excited about sex with Allen. We used to have a great sex life but now— all I ever think about is what's bugging me about him."

"Just for today," I said to her, "try thinking about all the nice things he's ever done for you. Try to think about what attracted you to him in the beginning. Focus on a few good things today and try to set everything else aside until five o'clock when Allen gets home."

The Language of Passion

Words are powerful agents in the sexual realm. Both Solomon and his new bride knew the value of a few kind words.

Solomon realized his young wife was insecure in her looks because she was tanned from the hard work of watching sheep in the fields. The women in Solomon's court were very light-skinned because they had been sheltered from the sun. The young wife also felt insecure about her station in life and her simple background. Solomon picked up on the anxieties of his wife and did two very specific things. First, he used language to build up her self-esteem, especially in the area of her beauty. Then he went out of his way to set up a lavish and very special setting for their intimate times together.

In turn, this bride sought out times to be with her husband. She made herself ready physically, emotionally and mentally. She spoke kind words, specifically chosen to build up her mate and draw him to her.

So, you may be asking what some of those tantalizing and alluring words were that the biblical lovers said to one another. What did their words mean in our language?

The Song of Songs is a beautiful word picture of intimate love. Many commentaries have been written in an attempt to capture the meaning of the poet. We (Bill and Pam) took our favorite commentary on our honeymoon. *Solomon on Sex* by Joseph Dillow comprehensively captures the flavor of romance we see in this Song of Songs. In this chapter, we will include a few of Dillow's highlights, along with those of other commentators, to help give a very literal interpretation of this romantic poem.

The uniqueness of the intimate relationship depicted in this book from the Bible, which sets it apart from love stories found on book racks, is that this book was penned by the inspiration of God. It elevates marital love and is sandwiched in the center of the Bible surrounded by other teaching on marriage pleasure. This is not an ideal from the mind of man that would lead to unreal comparisons. Rather, it is the portrait of two real people who loved God and tried to work out his principles for love.

The Husband's Words

Solomon begins by comparing his love to the things most cherished in his environment. Although women today may find his comparisons rather unusual, in his day they were the highest of compliments. He says, "I liken you, my darling, to a mare harnessed to one of the chariots of Pharaoh." Basically, this means she's one in million, like a handsome and flawless horse especially chosen for the king. She was chosen because she stood out from the crowd. He uses the very intimate term of *my darling*, which in those times had a two-fold meaning of "to guard or care for" and "to delight by sharing sex."[1]

What woman doesn't love being told she's one in a million? Any woman would be thrilled to hear that no one can hold a candle to her in her husband's eyes—and that just by looking at her, he desires to be with her sexually.

One day on our honeymoon, I (Pam) had just stepped from the shower and, looking into the mirror, I began to criticize my body. Bill was sitting on the bed, admiring his new wife. As I would comment on an area I thought needed improving, he would counter with how beautiful it was. This went on for a few minutes until he could stand it no longer. He was angry that I would put down his choice of a wife. I was not only tearing myself down but undermining Bill's taste. He stood up, wrapped his arms around me and told me to look straight into his eyes.

I complied, intrigued by the mystery of what my new husband was up to. He very seriously and very lovingly said, "I will be your mirror. My eyes will reflect your beauty. You are beautiful, Pamela. You are perfect, and if you ever doubt it, come stand before me. The mirror of my eyes will tell you the true story. You are perfect for me."

Over the last fourteen years, whenever self-doubt was looming on the horizon, through three pregnancies and baby blues, my mirror has never stopped telling me how perfect I am for him. Because of this continual confidence-building, I have grown more sexually adventurous. In Bill's eyes I am beautiful, and in his arms I am safe.

Just as Bill has continued to praise me, Solomon continues to praise his new bride. He says how beautiful she is by telling her, "Your eyes are doves."[2] This is a reference to her innocence and pure character, as the dove is often used as a symbol of virtue.

In chapter two he says she is "like a lily among thorns."[3] Now she's really standing out. All the other women are like thorns to him by comparison.

A few paragraphs later, Solomon very explicitly lists the alluring physical qualities of his bride from head to toe.

How beautiful you are, my darling! Oh, how beautiful! Your eyes behind your veil are doves. Your hair is like a flock of goats descending from Mount Gilead.[4]

This is his way of saying her hair was streaming beautifully down her body, and her beautiful, pure eyes were peeping from under her cascade of hair. The goats referred to here were animals with

glistening, silky black hair.[5]
Your teeth are like a flock of sheep just shorn, coming up from the washing. Each has its twin; not one of them is alone. Your lips are like a scarlet ribbon; your mouth is lovely.[6]
The reference to her teeth meant they were white and none were missing.[7] This makes sense because the next place Solomon looks is at her lovely mouth, which is compared to a scarlet thread. It is likely that Solomon is kissing and caressing as he continues his journey of admiration. He moves from gazing to foreplay at this point.
Your temples behind your veil are like the halves of a pomegranate. Your neck is like the tower of David, built with elegance; on it hang a thousand shields, all of them shields of warriors.[8]
"Temples like pomegranates" refers to her rosy cheeks. Her neck like a tower explains that he notices her queenly and erect posture. References to the shield give the idea that he looks to her for strength.
Your two breasts are like two fawns, like twin fawns of a gazelle that browse among the lilies.[9]
The reference to her breasts can be better understood by knowing more about gazelles. They are delicate animals, soft to touch and two-toned in color, a very white and a darker brown. They are frolicsome and playful, yet graceful and quiet. They were also served to kings as delicacies. With this in mind, Solomon was probably delighting in touching and kissing while he admired.[10] In Proverbs 5:18-19, Solomon writes wise words of advice, "Rejoice in the wife of your youth. . . . May her breasts satisfy you always, may you ever be captivated by her love."
Because men can find this area of a women's body playful yet calming, a variety of moods can be experienced while enjoying lovemaking. If a woman is held in respect and purity like the lily in Solomon's poetic line, her breasts will hold a continual en-

chantment for her husband throughout the years. Solomon does not rush the process, but continues the foreplay.

Until the day breaks and the shadows flee, I will go to the mountain of myrrh and to the hill of incense.[11]

This reference can be decoded by other references in this book. Female genitals are referred to as a garden, and the scents referred to are frankincense and myrrh.[12] Here, he begins genital foreplay. While he continues to caress, he continues to verbally express his love also:

All beautiful you are, my darling; there is no flaw in you. Come with me from Lebanon, my bride, come with me from Lebanon. Descend from the crest of Amana, from the top of Senir, the summit of Hermon, from the lions' dens and the mountain haunts of the leopards. You have stolen my heart, my sister, my bride; you have stolen my heart with one glance of your eyes, with one jewel of your necklace. How delightful is your love, my sister, my bride! How much more pleasing is your love than wine, and the fragrance of your perfume than any spice! Your lips drop sweetness as the honeycomb, my bride; milk and honey are under your tongue. The fragrance of your garments is like that of Lebanon.[13]

With descriptions of beautiful places, he tells her that she is totally beautiful. She makes his heart beat faster. Her love is better than wine. Her natural oils, or scent, are better than any scent in nature or made by man. The milk and honey under her tongue tell her that he loves her kisses. This may be a reference to deep "French" kissing as well.

You are a garden locked up, my sister, my bride; you are a spring enclosed, a sealed fountain. Your plants are an orchard of pomegranates with choice fruits, with henna and nard, nard and saffron, calamus and cinnamon, with every kind of incense tree, with myrrh and aloes and all the finest spices.[14]

This is an allusion to her garden again. The fact that he notes that the garden was sealed meant she had kept herself for him alone. All the references to plants were about fragrance-giving plants, so again he is complimenting her naturalness and the scent coming from her arousal as being very pleasing to him. It is apparent at this point that Solomon took his time, lavishing verbal praise while giving physical touch.

Scientific studies have clearly shown that the arousal time is different between men and women.[15] Women take longer to become aroused, and they also relax more slowly after lovemaking. Men arrive at sexual arousal much more quickly, then, almost immediately after intercourse, crash into a state of relaxed ecstasy. Since Solomon was careful to proceed at a rate comfortable to his wife, while he enveloped her in praise, he reaped the benefit of fulfilling sex as well.

The Wife's Words

This young bride also carefully uses verbal praise to encourage the heart of her husband.

She begins by expressing the overwhelming connection she feels toward her husband. She states, "My lover is to me a sachet of myrrh resting between my breasts."[16] The picture is that he lies close to her heart. Just as the fragrance of perfume lingers day and night, his love penetrates her heart with a strengthening aroma.[17] She adds that her beloved is a cluster of henna blossoms from En Gedi.[18] En Gedi is a lush oasis in the middle of a harsh desert.[19] Solomon's presence refreshes her.

She continues by telling her man how handsome he is and how much she enjoys their lovemaking quarters. When she says their couch is luxurious, she probably is noticing the silk or satin bed covering. She then describes the very beams which Solomon used to build her room. She notices the things he has done to prepare for their special time together. Noting the building process was a subtle way of saying thanks for his provision.

She exclaims that his banner over her is love. The king's banner was probably placed over the entrance to their bridal chamber and was a symbol of his protection and his secure love toward her. Because she needed reassurance of her place in his life due to her lowly background, this banner was a public display of his confident love for her. She is thrilled, and her exclamation is a way of saying, "I noticed! You care!"

Immediately, she says she is lovesick and desires him. Here she is fulfilling his desire and matching his arousal pattern. She recognizes the compliment of being told, "I want you and I want you now!"

She describes exactly how he is making love to her. "His left arm is under my head, and his right arm embraces me."[20] Clear communication can be a compliment in lovemaking. It's like saying "I love it when you . . ."

But this bride was not always so thoughtful. In a later encounter, her husband comes in late at night after a hard day of royal responsibility and she rebuffs him. He then leaves, placing myrrh on the door handle as a love note. She opens the door, her hand drips with myrrh and she is sorry. She looks for him but to no avail. Shortly afterward, we find her doing a very healthy thing, that is, musing on her lover while he is gone and thinking about how to make their next time together memorable:

My lover is radiant and ruddy, outstanding among ten thousand. His head is purest gold; his hair is wavy and black as a raven. His eyes are like doves by the water streams, washed in milk, mounted like jewels. His cheeks are like beds of spice yielding perfume. His lips are like lilies dripping with myrrh. His arms are rods of gold set with chrysolite. His body is like polished ivory decorated with sapphires. His legs are pillars of marble set on bases of pure gold. His appearance is like Lebanon, choice as its cedars. His mouth is sweetness itself; he is altogether lovely. This is my lover, this my friend, O daughters of Jerusalem.[21]

She says he is dazzling and ruddy—handsome and healthy. She also notes that he is outstanding among men. She comments on his raven-black hair and says the locks are like purest gold. She moves downward in her mind and remembers his dove-like eyes bathed in milk. This is one symbol of purity perched on another.

His cheeks are like beds of spice and his lips are lilies dripping with myrrh. The spice probably refers to the custom of perfuming the beard. The lilies are most likely red, and the myrrh refers to his sweet breath (often aided by the chewing of herbs).[22]

In her daydream she outlines his body. His arms are rods of gold set with chrysolite, meaning they are strong and have transparently pink nails. His body is ivory and inlaid with sapphires. Because of the carved reference, he was most likely fit and firm with muscular definition.

She goes down to his legs of marble set on bases of gold. The marble segment is most likely the part of the loin where the legs separate, and the pillars are his strong legs. The reference to choice cedars also shows her feelings of valuing his strength and masculinity.

Then she declares her adoration for his mouth of sweetness. She was attracted to him not just for his looks, but because of his gentle and kind words. She states very clearly the two reasons she misses him—"This is my lover, this is my friend."[23]

Men rarely confide how much they love it when their wives miss them sexually and are willing to be playful and pursue them. Most often, when a wife has lost the passion for her husband, the simplest solution is for her to slow down and think about her husband's positive attributes—and then let him know she wants him. In focusing on the good characteristics of her husband, sexual assertiveness rises up naturally, rather than by some stilted imitation or Hollywood-type acting.

On those rare days when life is a bit slower, it is easy for me

(Pam) to long for and pursue Bill because I have spent time quietly admiring him. On other, more hectic days, I have to choose to focus my distracted thoughts on Bill and my desire to be with him.

I have to plan to remember Bill romantically. His picture is on my key chain; I might give a quick "I love you" call to his office; when changing my clothes I might pull his suit out of his closet just to smell the remaining fragrance of his cologne; I keep the cards he's given me handy so I can reread one or two. But by far the best way to prepare my heart to enjoy Bill is to take a quiet minute in the car or at my desk, close my eyes and remember one of our special intimate moments. Choosing to set aside my distractions and focus my thoughts on Bill draws my heart to his.

After Solomon's wife spends the day dreaming of her love, she sets a game plan. Because she was the one who pushed him away, now she is the one to pursue.

When he enters, she is dancing. In the Hebrew culture, dancing is always connected with joy. The wife is joyous because her lover and friend is home. Solomon is overjoyed at the welcome. He verbally praises her (this time from the feet up) as she dances.[24]

She uses poetic language to invite her husband to come to the country and make love. "Come, my lover, let us go to the countryside, let us spend the night in the villages. Let us go early to the vineyards to see if the vines have budded, if their blossoms have opened, and if the pomegranates are in bloom—there I will give you my love."[25] The book ends after the lovers have spent time in the country. The final lines are from the wife to her husband:

"Come away, my lover, and be like a gazelle or like a young stag on the spice-laden mountains."

Passion Is Possible

"I just don't know what to make of Allen recently," Teresa whispered to me (Pam) only a few weeks after our phone conversation. "It's like he's a different person. He's been so nice. Last night was so . . ." She paused and smiled, looking at Allen with a sparkle in her eye as he stood across the room talking with Bill and a few other men. She sighed. She didn't have to tell me; I could tell by the dreamy smile on her face that they had had one of those special sexual times. Kind words had rekindled pleasure and passion, and with pleasure came renewed hope, and with hope came the opportunity for renewed love.

It's great to think about the love words in the Song of Songs and the moving honeymoon mirror experience of Bill and Pam, but what if you don't have those feelings? How can they be developed?

A few years ago, Sally was attacked by breast cancer. She had surgery, a modified radical mastectomy. Following was a year of intensive chemotherapy that totally zapped her physical strength. All during that time my sexual affection needed to be kept alive, because Sally had nagging questions about whether I would be sexually attracted to her after the radical surgery. It was and continues to be important to assure Sally that her appeal to me is more than breasts.

But first it was something I had to face with God. Could I love my wife after this type of surgery? God broadened my understanding of love and helped me focus on Sally's many other qualities; that focus in turn deepened my valuing of her and renewed our love in new dimensions. And I still treasure her physically, despite the changes brought by illness.

I've come to see that true romance comes from a deep valuing of the other person in dozens of areas. The problem with this generation is that they often limit loving to only the physical, never realizing that building the caring and serving part of the relationship is a sure-fire way to develop or restore the passion of a relationship.

Pleasure Point:

In a neutral place, such as a restaurant or a park, each partner should name areas of his or her body about which he or she feels inadequate. By talking about areas of felt inadequacy, you may discover your mate doesn't even notice or care that you have thick ankles, or stubby toes, or that you are a little rounder than the day you met.

You'll also want to discuss inhibitions you each have when you make love. Some of the most common for women are failure to reach orgasm, discomfort in intercourse and simply having a low sex drive due to feeling inadequate. For men premature ejaculation and inhibitions are most common. If these small problems are not addressed, then "frigidity" and "impotence" may follow. You may decide as a couple to seek medical advice. Ed Wheat has done an excellent series of cassettes describing common problems and solutions. Appendix B suggests a number of resources.

Often the remedy to dysfunction is found in a loving and accepting environment created by kind communication. Even in the case of a medical complication, solutions come easier in an accepting environment.

Over the next few days, each partner should prepare a "gift of praise" designed to encourage his or her mate in the area of insecurity. A few days later, at a predetermined date night, each partner gives his or her "gift of praise" to the other.

For example, if the wife feels inadequate about her breast size, the husband could center his lovemaking around the breasts, caressing and complimenting while making love.

Or if a husband is losing confidence, because of difficulty in maintaining an erection or having a slow ejaculation, the wife can focus on caressing and kissing all of her husband's body, including his penis. Her focus also should be on her appreciation of him as a person. She could connect physical and emotional attributes like, "I love your strong hands. They remind me of how safe I feel when I am being held in your arms."

10
THE
PLEASURE
OF
FUN

CINDIE AND I (PAM) STOOD SIP-
ping iced tea in her cozy kitchen. Conversations drifted like the
cool breeze on this hot summer day. Topics floated in and out:
the kids, shopping, meals, dreams.

"Bruce and I used to have so much fun," Cindie said. "I know
you wouldn't believe it to look at us now. Work, work, work.
That's all we do. The two jobs Bruce works keep us afloat, but
he's exhausted. And after chasing four little kids all day, I'm no
party animal either. We used to have parties and go out with
friends. Even after we had Ryan, we did fun things as a family,
but then the business went bad. I can't seem to have fun when
I feel broke."

Cindie shrugged her shoulders, let out a heavy sigh, crossed into the living room and collapsed onto her overstuffed sofa. She had the look of a dejected teen who had just been grounded.

She twirled a piece of her long auburn hair around her finger and looked into the air dreamily. "Sometimes I fantasize about having an affair with someone who is very rich, just to have some fun again. I want a guy to take me out shopping and spend a mint. For once, I would like to feel soft fur around my neck or a silk dress.

"I want to go to the theater, the movies, a nice dinner, and have men turn their heads because I walked in the room. The only heads turning now are when my two-year-old throws a tantrum in the grocery store. I want a guy to gaze at me."

Cindie sat up straight as if shocked out of her daydream. "Please don't say anything to Bruce. I love him too much. It would break his heart. I know it wouldn't be fun if it weren't Bruce. At least, that's what I keep telling myself." She sighed.

Give Me a Break!

Cindie is like many women and men who are several years into marriage and bored. She longs for the fun and thrill of less responsibility. Six out of ten in Generation X say they married for companionship,[1] yet when that friendship becomes stale they long to escape. Even though 85 percent believe that God intended marriage to last a lifetime, 74 percent say marriage should not limit their opportunities or activities.[2] If the thrill is gone, the marriage is next to go.

One common predicament that destroys marital joy is a man's mid-life crisis that usually hits when he is in his forties and trying to escape the pressures of life. Counsel that we (Jim and Sally) have given to many women whose husbands are in mid-life crisis is to remember "he wants his wife to be a girlfriend and a lover, not just a mother and a household manager."[3] "Be your husband's best friend. Understand what he's going through and attempt to meet his needs. In other words be fun and sexy not naggy or bossy."[4]

In an interview, I (Sally) shared how I personally handled Jim's crisis. "I began to think in terms of how a younger woman would act around him. I decided to look at him with the eyes of a twenty-two-year-old and tell him what I saw in him and how I felt about him. I wanted to affirm him more and act more flirtatious."[5]

Women, too, have a crisis time in their late thirties when they desire a break from overwhelming responsibilities. Their marriage seems stale and their husband inattentive. "It isn't that they hate each other; it isn't that they don't love each other. They are just apathetic. They are bored, bored, bored."[6]

Even though the situation often seems stale, marriages at this stage have great potential since both the husband and wife are looking for friendship, flirting and fun. The couple has a great opportunity to invest in their relationship and arrive at a deeper level of fulfillment and enjoyment.

Tragically, many are choosing to engage in a desperate hunt for a self-centered fix of fun that may lead to an affair. If a husband and wife keep dating each other, they will sail more smoothly through the different stages of marital life. Every enjoyable memory and each fun activity is like a deposit into your marital bank account where the interest mounts and the dividends pay well.

Date Your Way Out of the Doldrums

Doug Fields, author of *Creative Romance*, notes, "Many couples have lost the spark they shared before they married and have replaced it with a humdrum routine. I'm convinced that lack of dating and romance in marriage is one of the major causes of a broken relationship."[7]

Date nights give you something to look forward to, something exciting to anticipate. Marriage counselor Norman Wright suggests couples kick-start a bored marriage with "cherishing days." The couple begins by each making a list of things the other could do to make him or her feel special or cherished. Then for several days each partner lavishes these acts of romance and kindness on the other with no accounting of who did what for whom. They immerse themselves in the simple enjoyment derived from pleasing the other spouse.[8]

After this initial round of romance, you'll be ready to enjoy some good, healthy fun with your lover. Each can make a list of activities you think would be fun. Compare notes and start living it up. Don't be afraid to get out of your comfort zone.

A wife may not think going to the Indy 500 is fun, but if she concentrates on helping her honey have a blast while he's there, the enjoyment will be contagious. Bill thought the words "ballet" and "boredom" were synonyms the first year we were married, but having danced and competed in gymnastics for years, I wanted Bill to share in my world, so in a very giving moment, Bill let me teach him how to do the lifts and catches of ballet. After dropping me a few times, and after a lot of laughs, Bill came to appreciate ballet. Now a Christmas rarely goes by without a trip to "The Nutcracker." Because of Bill's desire to understand me and my world, I love to dance into his arms. I am also willing to take a trek into his world to do some things I used to call boring.

Sometimes finding things in common is a hit-and-miss proposition. When failures arise, just laugh and try something else. If your tastes in pleasure run in opposing directions, try things neither of you have ever experienced to see if you can find a new common denominator.

We (Bill and Pam) always have a running list of dream dates we'd love to do: hot air ballooning, backpacking as a couple in the wilds, having lunch in a garden cafe, spending the day in an art museum, or learning to sail. We may or may not end up completely liking them, but we'll have fun on the adventure.

Cheap Thrills

We have a weekly date night so we can touch base. These dates are not extravagant but are pockets of carefree fun in our very responsible world. They take us away from the kids and home repairs and committee meetings for a little while. We like to do things such as walk to the ice cream store, rent a tear-jerker movie from the forties, stroll the beach, play a board game or shop for pajamas!

When the budget is really tight, we pull out our list of free or nearly free activities and pick one:

☐ A candlelight picnic at a park or the beach.

☐ A photo date where we take pictures of each other at our favorite romantic spot. If finances permit we take them to a one-hour developing place. Often we pick them up later, make a special frame or postcard and send them to one another.

☐ A drive, bike ride or walk to an inexpensive ice-cream store or fancy coffee shoppe.

☐ Hiking in a meadow or swinging at a park while we take turns listing A to Z why we love our mate.

☐ A mall walk. The goal is not to buy anything—only test perfume and cologne along the way!

☐ A squirt-gun or water fight.

☐ A car rally or treasure hunt where clues are written on hearts. The date consists of gathering clues to find the romantic hideaway, chocolate treat or other reward.

☐ Getting poetry books from the library and reading to one another. Some of our favorites are by Robert and Elizabeth Barrett Browning.

☐ Dinner in an unusual place, like our roof, a freeway overpass or a beach jetty. We get extra points if we compose a song or poem for the date.

☐ Reenacting a portion of a great romantic drama. Shakespeare's *Romeo and Juliet* is a great place to begin.

☐ Spending the day in bed. Breakfast in bed, piles of magazines, soft music (warning: you might not get in much reading).

☐ Reminiscing over our wedding album and early pictures or yearbooks.

☐ Reading a book on romance and marriage together. (Try *Solomon on Sex* by Joseph Dillow, *Romancing your Marriage* by H. Norman Wright or *Traits of a Lasting Marriage* by Jim and Sally Conway.)

☐ A living-room luau, Oriental evening or other ethnic treat.

☐ Renting an old-fashioned romance video from the forties and pulling out the tissue for a good cry together.

☐ Robbing the kids' toy chest and doing some one-on-one basketball, skateboard or suction-cup archery practice.

☐ Working out together. (Go for a jog, do aerobics to a video, visit a gym on a guest pass.)

☐ Baking or cooking something extravagant together. We give bonus points for cleaning up together.

☐ Playing computer games or board games. To have a variety, we borrow from friends.

☐ Flying a kite.

Perhaps not all the ideas on our list will appeal to you and your spouse. Be creative in making a list especially for *you!*

Look for the Unique

Find activities you both really enjoy. Look for ones you can do regularly that will also make you laugh. Your friends or work associates may find you strange, but go ahead and enjoy. For example, Bill changes from a suit and tie and I drop my books and papers for our almost daily half-hour of rollerblading! We get some puzzled looks as friends and neighbors drive by and realize that those two on the blades are the Farrels! The speed racing, trick skating and gliding hand-in-hand down the street is a welcome relief—even the stumbles and falls make us giggle like grade-schoolers.

Chuck and Cynthia Swindoll have taken up motorcycle riding. Chuck comments on their first visit to a Harley shop in his book, *Laugh Again.* He says, "We sat there and giggled like a couple of high-school sweethearts sipping a soda through two straws. She liked the feel of sitting close to me (she couldn't resist, naturally), and I liked the feel of her behind me and that giant engine underneath us. And that inimitable Harley roar. Man, it was great!

"Suddenly, sitting on that shiny black heritage Softail Classic with thick leather saddlebags, we were on the back streets of Houston in 1953 all over again, roaring to a Milby High School football game. She was wearing my letterman's sweater and red-and-white saddle oxfords, and I had a flattop with a ducktail and a black leather jacket with fringe and chrome studs!"[9]

That's a far cry from their everyday world. Chuck has been senior pastor of a large church, an author and a radio personality. Cynthia is the executive vice president of a radio broadcast ministry.

One couple we (Bill and Pam) know shoots skeet. Another skis. A third bought a trampoline. They say it was for the kids but we think they have as much fun as their children!

There are many ways to have fun. We (Jim and Sally) have spent a week rafting in the Grand Canyon. We also have soared over Napa Valley, snorkeled in the Caribbean and Pacific, and had many other once-in-a-lifetime experiences that drew us together.

However, we also find that ordinary events can become our unique fun that cements our relationship. We recently had our first small tomato from the single plant we've grown in a pot on our patio. We very carefully divided it between the two of us and put the sections on top of our salads, making much ado about our homegrown tomato.

We are at a time in our marriage when we take the liberty to do carefree things we couldn't do when we were younger. Routine errands turn into outings together, with the freedom to go farther, stay longer and do the unplanned if we want. While out, we decide to go look at used cars, drive through a new housing area or get an ice cream soda. We don't have to be at home to make sure the kids are safe and doing their homework. Neither do we have to be there to feed the dog. (She died about the same year the kids left home, and our cat eats whenever she pleases.)

We think it's fun to eat at an inexpensive place and split the meal between us. By sharing, we get all we should eat and then we can afford to do it more often. (We also like to eat at elegant restaurants at the ocean for special occasions!)

Because we are grandparents, we get true delight from playing with our grandchildren. They all live hundreds of miles away, in three directions, so whenever we get a speaking invitation near them, we are sure to accept. After our conference, it's "play time!" Our grandkids revive our spirit of fun as we play imaginary games, hide-and-seek, board games, croquet. Building with Legos helps us get a child's view of the world. That's a good break from the adult grind.

Jim and I also like to have what we call "adventures." These are usually the result of something not working out right. We may have decided to drive on an unpaved road as a shortcut to a destination. It turns out to be very rough or even hazardous. We may even end up not getting to where we were going. No matter, we've had a great adventure!

The Bible says, "A cheerful heart is good medicine."[10] And medical science has proved that to be true. Ten seconds of hard belly laughing raises the heart rate to the same level reached in ten minutes of strenuous rowing.[11] Laughter also creates natural endorphins, which act as pain relievers and make us feel better physically.[12] Laughter just makes life less grim.

To keep the air a little lighter around the Farrel house, we keep on hand several good, clean joke books.[13] We also have a running game of who can be the "punniest" and make a play on words in everyday conversation. We also hide squirt guns around the house, preloaded for a spontaneous water fight. (Our kids are especially eager to initiate these.) And yes, we confess, we've even had a food fight or two.

One couple we know is always playing practical jokes on each other. They get away with it because each one is careful not to allow the jokes to get out of hand and hurt the feelings or reputation of the partner.

A Fun Investment

We encourage couples to invest in their marriage in the same way they invest in a home. Set money aside for dates, getaways, anniversary celebrations and romantic treats. One couple, whose children have entered the teen years, added a romantic hideaway to their home with a hot tub and plenty of privacy. Marriage counselor Norman Wright and his wife created a mountain retreat in the back yard of their Los Angeles home, complete with a waterfall.[14]

For you, the investment may be:

☐ Gourmet cookware
☐ A pool
☐ A volume of poetry
☐ His and her fishing rods
☐ Guitar lessons so you can serenade each other
☐ Ballroom dance lessons
☐ A tennis club membership
☐ Two round trip tickets to anywhere you can be alone!

Don't let cost become the issue. Our rollerblades and protective gear were relatively inexpensive. If we prorate the cost of the skates over a two-year period, it's less than fifty cents a day. If we

pay a baby sitter and go somewhere other than surrounding side-
walks to skate, the date still runs under five dollars. The bonus
is that it also helps us win a victory over the battle of the bulge!

Creative date specialists Doug Fields and Todd Temple have
written several books packed with great dating ideas. They say
dating one's mate does several things for a relationship. It is an
antidote to boredom. It stores up memories. It provides an escape from the commonplace and predictable. They recommend
that a great romantic date be personal, such as making reservations at your mate's favorite restaurant or having his or her favorite dessert on hand.[15] To get ideas for your creative dating list,
look in three places: the future, the past and now.

Look to the Future
To build memories to get you through a hectic time, or before
an extended period where you may have to be separated, plan
a "night to remember."

Use the "Flashback" method. The date is filled with terrific first
impressions so later you two can flash back and savor those
romantic moments. For example, play a new, romantic CD. Adorn
yourself in a new outfit, complete with new perfume or after-
shave. Dine on new exotic foods and perhaps capture it all in a
snapshot.[16]

On each of our birthdays (Bill and Pam) we take turns creating
a lasting memory for each other. Most years we have a very small
budget. One very stressful year, I (Pam) was a re-entry college
student with two toddlers, and very pregnant. We were building
a home and we were in a new ministry. Bill knew I needed an
escape. Our home was half-built. My schooling was half-done. My
pregnancy was half-over. We were weary and in desperate need
of a second wind.

Bill conspired with Beth, a friend of mine. She arranged twenty-
four hours at a beach condo. I was whisked off the house build-

ing site in my overalls. Beth packed a picnic basket and delivered it to the condo ahead of time. She then cared for the kids overnight as Bill and I let the rolling waves of the ocean usher new romance into our life. That twenty-four hours was an oasis in a desert of overwhelming responsibilities.

In prior years I (Bill) have been known to write a song, take Pam on a treasure hunt or make our room into a bed-and-breakfast when I saw a hectic schedule on the horizon ahead.

If your life is nothing but pressure, you may want to plan a getaway like one we (Pam and Bill) went on recently. We arranged child care, purchased two tickets to a favorite concert and got an amazing hotel deal from the local visitors' bureau. We spent three wonderful days and two nights in a hotel on an ocean bay. We purposely slept in, awaking each day to *no plans!* Great memories were made.

Look Back

You can go the other route and relive some of the highlights of your marriage. Travel to the place of your first meeting or your first date. Enjoy some of the activities you did as newlyweds. Reread love letters, browse through photo albums or watch the video of your wedding.

Remember the day you first met, your first date, when you first knew you were in love. What were the characteristics that drew you to your mate? What were the things you enjoyed most about those dating days? Was it the long walks? The long heart-to-heart talks? The love letters? The time on the phone? If some of these things are missing lately, plan to work them into your life again. Make a list of your favorite early dates. Are there common threads that run through them? Weave the tapestry of your love by creating a walk down memory lane.

We (Jim and Sally) relish our early dating memories. We were college students together. Now Jim is on the Board of Trustees for that same school, so we are back on campus once or twice a year. What fun we have, seeing our old haunts and recollecting those happy times—the sunken garden where we had our first long talk about spiritual matters, the laundry room window Jim knew would be open when I missed curfew and got locked out of my dorm, the sidewalk where we surreptitiously engraved our initials in wet cement.

As we continue our walk around memory lane, we see the tree in the middle of campus where one balmy spring night Jim asked if I'd like to have a ring. When I said yes, he reached into his shirt pocket and pulled out a piston ring!

A few days later, before we parted for summer break, Jim drove me to the little lake we often visited. Under a now famous tree, he gave me a box containing a soft stuffed horse. I thought it was nice he was giving me something to remember him by during the time we would be apart.

"Look closer!" he urged. When I did, I couldn't believe my eyes. Attached to the horse's nose was a diamond ring!

That tree became a landmark. Jim took my picture there that day. After we were married and had our first daughter, we returned to take our picture by the tree again. When we went back with our second daughter, we arrived just after a storm and found our beloved tree had toppled. We took a picture by the uprooted end and adopted a nearby tree under which we later took a picture when our family was complete with three daughters. In recent years we have taken another picture—just the two of us again visiting our special spot.

We have found that recalling moments from the past strengthens our ties. We realize no one else could understand the full meaning of those incidents. Those unique times in history and never-to-be-repeated stages of our lives, those exclusive experiences, can never be repeated. To us they are invaluable and irreplaceable!

In our (Bill and Pam's) dating days in college, we both lived with college roommates. Because we desired to stay pure in our sex life, our dates were commonly held at the very public park around the corner from the apartment where Pam lived. We walked, jogged, did the par course, played basketball, had picnics, biked to the park, sat on the swings and talked for hours.

Our other special getaway was the beach, near where Bill was a college student. Today we count it a special blessing to live near another beach. Bill can serenade me by a beach fire, or we can stroll in the moonlight and quietly remember the early moments, conversations and decisions that knit us together.

The other special memory we have from our early dating days is the pattern we had of serving others together. Fortunately, we decided early to work together as well as play. It was common for us to babysit, help out in the youth group, teach or counsel together. We enjoyed helping others as a team. Working together is fun for us.

During the course of counseling engaged and newly married couples, we often get to relive those early dating days. Writing a book on pleasure and passion also has its advantages. Our "breaks" are very active and interesting! At those times it sure doesn't feel like work!

Look at Now
No matter how precious the past is, you can't stay there. It is meant to be used as a snapshot into your love, a reminder to jog your romantic memories. To constantly dwell in the past is unhealthy. It would be easy to compare the good old days to the hectic new days. That isn't the purpose of building memories. Rather, good memories can be a catalyst to remind you to *carpe diem*, "seize the day."

Spontaneity is one of the quickest ways to rev up the romantic life. Buy a rose from a corner vendor. Tell your wife she is looking sexy to you. Grab a quick kiss in the kitchen. Whisper to your spouse, "I really want you *right now.* The kids are busy playing, so let's . . ."

Give compliments as they pop into your head. Don't be discouraged if your mate seems caught off guard by this sudden burst of spontaneity. Don't be hurt if a few of your sexual advances are rebuffed. As you keep it up, your mate will begin to believe you really are serious about having fun on the spur of the moment. Your spouse might surprise you in return and ask if you want to camp out under the stars. You could get a phone call with an alluring invitation to a secluded lunch. You may even get a hotel key dropped off at your office. Everyone likes surprises, especially when they are personally tailored to meet your needs.

Do something completely bizarre. Eat dinner out of a picnic basket while you watch the sunset from your rooftop. Rent a limo and drive through town. Have your teens serve you dinner on white linen and china in front of your fireplace.

Take turns planning and surprising your mate on date nights. Set a budget for dates so it doesn't become a contest that leads you into debt. You may not be able to go to the tropics today, but you could borrow a lot of plants and have a garden patio dinner. Splurging for a hammock to sleep in together would add authenticity to the pretend Caribbean getaway.

Flexibility is the key. We have a phrase at our house: "Blessed are the flexible for they shall not be broken." If it's not the perfect dream date, go with the flow. Mistakes and mishaps can be turned into magic.

Once I planned to whisk Bill away from the office for a romantic country picnic. He knew that I was going to stop by at noon. I had noted a space of two hours in his calendar and had confirmed it that morning. However, when I arrived, I found that a key church leader was having a crisis and in fifty minutes the gentleman would be there for counsel. Undaunted, I locked the office doors,

turned on some soft music, told the secretary to hold his calls—
and we had a nice, though quick, romantic lunch in his office.

Perseverance pays off. I could have chosen to get my feelings
hurt and pout over a lost dream, but I didn't think it was profitable to use up precious time together complaining that we don't
have enough time together!

Be My Valentine
The Farrels' favorite Valentine date was when we were struggling
students and had less than ten dollars for the entire evening. Ten
dollars had to cover gifts, dinner and activities. We divided up the
letters in the word *valentine* and each of us took half the letters
and half the money. Bill asked to arrange the food so I donated
a few bucks from my share to him.

"V" was for a vase with hand-picked flowers for Pam.

"A" was for "act": we acted out Romeo and Juliet's love scene
on a park stage with nobody watching.

"L" was for laugh as Bill read jokes out of a library book.

"E" was for eat—sausage on a stick from the mall while we
window shopped.

"N" was for nostalgia as we dropped off Pam's wedding ring
at the jewelry store to have it cleaned.

"T" was for tapes: we went to a music store and listened to
demo tapes of our favorite musicians.

"I" was for ice cream.

"N" was for a nighttime drive.

"E" was for entertainment, when Bill read Pam a love poem
while we parked overlooking the lights of the city.

Each letter was a new surprise to the other person, so the
evening was definitely an adventure!

The Big Payoff
The great thing about romantic adventures is that they can start

anytime you're ready to invest a little time and energy. The last time we had dinner with Bruce and Cindie, the couple we spoke of at the beginning of the chapter, things were looking much brighter to Cindie.

"We are remaking our bedroom into a Victorian bed-and-breakfast room, like our honeymoon suite at the inn," smiled Cindie as she gazed across the table at Bruce.

"I rearranged some funds and we bought trail bikes so we can go exploring now too." Bruce winked at Cindie at the mention of exploring. "I didn't think I could carve out the time, but one day I realized I just had to make some time. The last thing I wanted to do was lose Cindie."

Pleasure Point:

Brainstorm together and make a list of dating ideas. Begin with these questions:

☐ Is there anything you liked to do as a kid that you would like to do as a couple?

☐ Before you met your mate, what was your favorite leisure activity?

☐ List the romantic spots from your early dating life.

☐ Name five places you would like to go if time and money were not a factor.

☐ Name five things you would like to do that cost less than $5.00.

Establish a weekly date night. Each of you choose an activity from your list for the next two dates.

11
THE
PLEASURE
OF
DECISIVENESS

THE PARTY WAS UPBEAT. LIVELY music and colorful streamers blowing in the breeze made a perfect setting for this young, energetic crowd. The faces were fresh and alive. Conversations spontaneously erupted. The room was decorated with sharp-looking people wearing fashionable clothes and natural smiles. Everyone seemed so together.

Heather moved across the crowded room. Clutching my arm, she frantically whispered in my ear, "Pam, tell Bill he has to talk to Justin. I'm going crazy. He can't decide on anything! He changes jobs like other people change clothes.

"I want kids, but financially we can't handle it because of his flakiness. Now, he is even thinking about having Tony move in with us to pay half the rent." She grabbed me with such urgency that her long nails dug into my arm. "Please—maybe Bill can get through to him!"

As I gave Heather a hug, I saw Bill across the room. When I moved near him, I recognized he was already deep in conversation with Justin, a young professional in his early thirties.

"Heather is driving me crazy!" Justin had begun. "It's like she's switched personalities or something. When we were dating, she was so much fun. Now she's so depressed.

"When I ask her what's wrong, she says she doesn't know. The house is a wreck. She mopes around all day. I keep asking her if it's me—something I did. She says no. When I ask what's wrong, she just answers, 'You wouldn't understand.'

"How can I understand something she won't talk about? I wonder if she even knows what's wrong with herself. I love her, Bill. I can't stand to see her like this. What can I do? I think it has something to do with her stepdad. He's kind of a pervert if you ask me."

We have found that one of the most common patterns for couples who are carrying old emotional wounds is a strange inability to make wise decisions. Three of the most common sources of these wounds are:

1. The pressure of competition
2. Dysfunctional family background
3. Past abusive experiences

Wounds inflicted by these influences seem to erupt from nowhere. A couple may be going along just fine, then boom! out of left field comes some emotional upheaval that knocks out their emotional stability. These emotional land mines *can* be removed and a couple *can* stop the destruction to their relationship.

The Pressure of Competition
This generation is in competition with itself as well as with the

older parent generation. By age thirty-five, they want to have all that their parents have achieved in a whole lifetime.

These characteristics appear in two groups of people. First, there are the *overachievers* who are applauded by the older generation. "You're doing great. Keep it up." Two full-time jobs, marriage, three kids, a giant mortgage on a new home, payments on two new cars, plus membership in several clubs, and music, ballet and gymnastics lessons for the kids.

These overachievers are apt to hit the wall in their early forties with a massive mid-life crisis. They will then ask, "Why have I been doing all of this?"

They are likely to break their marriage and desire to drop out of the rat race—never realizing that all along they have been competing with their parents. But the evaluation and rethinking of life will be very positive. It is only too bad that they were too busy in their twenties and thirties to be reflective, to modify their lifestyles and save their marriages.

The second group affected by the competition in this generation are the *underachievers.* Justin is so afraid of failure that he does not commit to anything. The person who is afraid of failure unconsciously reasons, "If I don't invest my emotions in this project or person, then I won't be hurt when it fails—and it will fail."

Shortly after he dropped out of college, Justin said to Heather, "Life is too short to spend time in school, let's just have fun." In his mid-twenties at the time, Justin hadn't maintained any significant commitments. He quit school. Then he quit a series of part-time jobs when they interfered with recreation or social plans. He had also quit on a series of deeply involved relationships when more commitment was desired by the woman.

Heather was attracted to Justin because of his free lifestyle. He seemed so happy and easygoing. Heather thought Justin would really love her because he was not weighed down with all of society's trappings.

"Why bother," Justin would tell her. "I see everyone killing themselves to make a buck. What for? Money doesn't seem to make anyone happy. It's like the world's all gonna end anyway—what's the use?"

Justin and Heather married in their mid-twenties, but neither of them really knew what they wanted to do with their lives. They had developed a pattern of indecision.

Many have been trained by the free-love movement to have Justin's freewheeling attitude toward responsibility. It is a "Don't Worry—Be Happy" mentality. These young adults hit their twenties with little guidance on how to be responsible in work, school, community or relationships.

Past failure to commit can lead to a pattern of poor personal choices where consequences are not considered or understood. The longer the indecisive pattern is maintained, the more permanent the damage to decision-making. The individual may begin to second-guess vital decisions, thinking, *After all, if I can't decide who I love and what I want to do about it, maybe I shouldn't decide other important things, or at least not decide them yet.* It's as if a permanent procrastination has set in.

If a couple does eventually marry after this yo-yo pattern, they may make the commitment because they have a "habit" of being together, rather than because they feel motivated to fulfill each other's needs. This same couple may also exhibit a tentativeness toward all family and couple decisions. Instead of making clear, thoughtful, decisive moves that produce a more productive and beneficial lifestyle, they simply let life happen to them.

The Dysfunctional Family Background

Emotional wounds are also common when one or both marriage partners have been raised in a severely troubled home. The husband or wife is often codependent with a parent rather than living interdependently with his or her spouse. When this happens, it is like three people trying to dance together with the third party leading. Life becomes very clumsy as they trip over each other's emotional baggage.

When there has been dysfunction in a family (often caused by alcohol, drug abuse, parental divorce or harmful parental patterns passed down through generations), negative relationship patterns have to be unlearned.

Chari is an example of the negative effects of being raised in a dysfunctional home. She came to me (Sally) for help. Chari was raised by an alcoholic father. Her father was a manager in a large corporation and did very well in his career. However, to relieve the stress of climbing the corporate ladder, he drank heavily and passed out on the couch most evenings. Weekends were unpredictable at Chari's home because she never knew if her dad would be drunk or not.

When he wasn't drinking, Chari's father wanted the very best for his children. His care often extended into unreal expectations. Chari found herself always trying to please her father, yet never quite being able to gain his approval. At the same time, his emotional aloofness and undependability caused by alcohol (and a subsequent divorce) made Chari lose respect for him.

She was caught in a vicious cycle of trying to please her father who was emotionally absent in her life. She had no respect for the man, yet she loved him because he was her dad.

To protect herself, Chari became emotionally distant from people. She longed for male companionship, yet she mistrusted men. As a teen, she found herself giving sex to gain love—but exiting the relationship before she could be hurt. Now, as a young adult, she had a desire to commit to her boyfriend, but she was paralyzed by fear. As Chari and I talked over a period of months, she began to see that she was reacting to present-day men on the basis of experiences with men in her past. She realized she needed a totally new pattern and gradually began to relate to men in healthy ways.

There's an Abuser in My Closet

Another cause of emotional wounds that disrupt marriages is abuse in many forms. Because of the lack of sexual restrictions in society, an overwhelming number of people have experienced some form of sexual assault. The assault may be child abuse by a parent, relative, friend or neighbor. Or it may be date rape or assault by a stranger. Various forms of sexual harassment can also cause deep distress.

If any of these episodes happened prior to marriage and have not been resolved, the baggage is then carried into marriage. Feelings toward the abuser may be turned against the spouse, as a substitute abuser. The spouse becomes distressed, trying to figure out what motivated this negative behavior, when he or she may have done nothing to deserve this treatment.

Heather knew she wasn't treating Justin right, but she wasn't able to stop. She was so depressed that she didn't want to get out of bed. But she also wanted to know exactly what time Justin would be home. If anything unexpectedly came up and he was late, she flew into an angry rage. In her anger, she would yell hurtful things at Justin, such as "You don't love me" and "You don't care at all what I feel!"

Sex was less and less enjoyable. She loved Justin and wanted to be close to him, but the thought of sex, especially if Justin initiated it, was repulsive. She felt as if she were going crazy.

"Justin, I love you too much to keep going like this. I have to get help. *We* have to get help!"

In Heather's first session she learned she wasn't crazy, but that her behaviors were a result of sexual abuse by her stepfather, complicated by a date rape. Her negative reactions were tied to men outside her marriage.

"It's as if the men I loathed were hiding in my closet," Heather said.

All these negative forces working against a marriage almost

invariably produce two common results.

Lack of Confidence

The first common result of emotional wounds is *a lack of confidence*. At this point, the relationship can be lost altogether because one or both of the partners may get fed up with the rollercoaster ride of emotions.

Emotional wounds can attack the very core of a person, sapping self-esteem. A loss of confidence can affect job performance, economic decisions and marital satisfaction. With the loss of confidence can come a loss of sexual confidence as well.

People who have been abused, or raised in a dysfunctional home, or are defeated by competition, are especially vulnerable to feelings of low self-esteem. Life paralyzes them as they bounce between fear and perfectionism.

They are hesitant to make decisions and take risks for fear they will fail. Once the courage is found to take a risk, crippled individuals then try too hard, thinking, *If I'm going to do this, I must do it right!* The definition of what is right is so distorted by low self-esteem that nothing short of perfection will do. When these individuals realize their efforts are not perfect, the old sense of failure kicks in and fear takes over.

Hi, Honey, We're Home

Sometimes a couple with unresolved past baggage will invite a third party into their relationship, move back home with parents or get involved in an affair. The cause is still the same—insecurity because of negative past experiences.

Justin came to me (Bill) one day with an interesting dilemma.

"We want to be out on our own," Justin said. "But we can never seem to pull it together financially. For the last three years, it's been like a yo-yo. We keep moving in and out of Heather's parents' house. We're tired of that. Not much privacy either. We're thinking about moving into an apartment with Tony and sharing expenses. What do you think?"

I asked Justin how he and Heather would protect their identity as a couple. What provisions and plans had they made to protect their privacy, especially since they were newlyweds?

"I hadn't thought about that," Justin said. "I guess we'll just work it out as we go. Tony will understand. He's a really good friend."

Justin was noticeably uncomfortable at this point and made up a reason why he had to leave immediately. He had already made up his mind that Tony would be their roommate.

They all moved in together two weeks later. And they were all disappointed in three months when it didn't work out. Justin and Heather moved back in with Heather's parents until they could find something better.

Justin and Heather lack a "couple" identity; they see themselves as singles who are married. Most often they are insecure about their future, economically and emotionally, and this arrangement allows them to put off facing their married responsibilities.

This third-party arrangement is most damaging to newlywed couples, because their sexual adjustment and privacy needs are deferred. Intimate communication and sexual expression are either curbed, which hurts the couple, or blatantly displayed before the single roommate or parents, which can cause further feelings of isolation and inadequacy.

Often couples cite economic necessity as a cause for this arrangement. Economic stress sometimes is the case, but often the couple is living above their means because money is not real to them—it's only a plastic credit card. They may place gadgets and recreation above the creative intimacy of sexual oneness which could be pursued by being in their own home.

If economic necessity is truly a factor, safeguards should be placed on the sanctity of the marital union. The couple should have definite private areas in the parental house or the shared apartment. Marriage is not a communal event. Above all, *this arrangement should be as temporary as possible.*

The problem is not primarily economic. It is the inability to make confident decisions that strengthen married "coupleness."

Lack of Leadership

The second common result of emotional wounds is *the inability to lead.* Overall ambivalence and tentativeness set in when there have been emotional wounds. This indecisiveness affects all of life. Their children also learn poor decision-making patterns by watching their parents waver and wander through life. When the dating years come, many parents, accustomed to indecisiveness, simply throw up their hands in despair, offering little concrete advice or guidance to their children in this most crucial relationship decision.

I (Pam) overheard a mother at a youth sporting event who was caught in this perplexing dilemma. She exclaimed to a whole bleacher full of parents, "I hope my daughter does better than I did. She's only in junior high. She told her boyfriend she didn't want to kiss him. Then she told me she wanted to wait until she was married to have sex. I told her, 'Good luck. I hope you do better than your mother!' "

Surgery for Emotional Wounds

No matter how the emotional wounds developed in your relationship—because of the pressure of competition, dysfunction or abuse—here are a few key steps that can release your marriage from their grasp.

1. Identify the source. Does your lack of marital unity spring from either the husband's or wife's upbringing? Does the hurt come from unhealthy friendships, distorted patterns of decision-making, physical, emotional, or sexual abuse from a family member or an outside sexual assault or rape? It is essential not only to identify the source but also to seek healing for that hurt. Many good resources are available through books, audio and video tapes, as well as professional counseling.

2. Choose to get well. In *Adult Children of Legal and Emotional Divorce,* Jim encourages people to say to themselves, " This is the year I'm going to get better. This is the week I'm going to get started."[1]

Don't view yourself as a victim. "Deciding to be healed is frightening. Many people choose just to live with life as it is instead of going through the process of healing."[2] You can choose the road of recovery that leads to a satisfying life. You can make a choice to listen to positive information through books and tapes and surround yourself with a support group that will encourage wellness. You are the one who can decide to get competent counsel from a trained pastor or counselor. Getting well *is your choice.*

3. Forgive any third party involved. The purpose of extending forgiveness to this third party is not to let him or her off the hook. Rather, it is to acknowledge that the offense was indeed a wrong suffered. Freedom can be experienced when you release the expectations you have for that person to make things right. Neil Anderson, author of *The Bondage Breaker,* acknowledges that "Forgiveness is costly; we pay the price of the evil we forgive. Yet you're going to live with those consequences whether you want to or not; your only choice is whether you will do so in the bitterness of unforgiveness or the freedom of forgiveness."[3]

It is helpful for both the husband and wife to make a list of third parties who need to be forgiven. Then, as a couple, place an empty chair for the imaginary guilty party to sit in. One person at a time, read the list, saying "I forgive you" to each offense.

Next, pray and thank God for giving you the will to forgive. Finally, destroy the paper. This exercise is helpful because you each may be allowing a third party or parties to control your emotional heartstrings if you are harboring bitterness.

Jan and Don Frank, in *When Victims Marry,* outline a helpful recovery process. This process includes confronting the issue, experiencing feelings brought on by the attack and acknowledging symptoms of current, related problems. Practical steps of forgiveness are coupled with guidelines for deciding whether to confront the offender in person or to pursue legal recourse, then rebuilding from that point.[4]

This can be a difficult process; it often requires a counselor as a guide. We have included resources in appendix B for more help in this area.

Recovery Pays Off

No matter how heinous the victimization was, it is possible to learn to free your marriage from its tentacles. Don Frank has this note of encouragement, "As you and your wife begin this process, take heart. Things do get better. You must be committed and prepared to give it time. We have reaped the benefits and have seen God's promise in Jeremiah 30:17 come to pass: 'I will restore you to health and heal your wounds.' "[5]

Couples who make the investment in weeding out the baggage caused by emotional wounds of the past will reap benefits from their diligence. The sacrifice of time, money for resources and counseling, and emotional energy will be worth it as the fruits of intimate pleasure grow and ripen in your marriage.

We (Jim and Sally) have seen the rewards of getting rid of the garbage from Jim's dysfunctional parental family that had affected our marriage. We know many cases (our own included) where recovery efforts are worth all the agony and pain it takes.

Working at recovery is like getting an unhealthy appendix removed. The surgery is painful, but without surgery the appendix may fester until it bursts and spreads poison throughout the body. Treatment is then even more severe and sometimes cannot prevent death. How much better to deal with the problem than to try to hide or ignore it, letting it fester until it blows up and causes greater problems.

Two Shall Become One

Heather and Justin stopped by our home after they'd been on a date.

"We were just out for dinner and we wanted to stop and say thanks for all your help and counsel this past year. We feel like a real couple now," Justin said to Bill.

"And we get to go back to our cozy little apartment and we will be *all alone!*" exclaimed Heather.

"No Tony, no mom or dad, just us. It's great!" Justin said as he hugged Heather.

As they walked down the driveway toward the car, Justin said, "Bill, we told some friends how the things you've shared with us have helped our marriage. They'll be giving you a call."

As they waved goodby, we knew they were now on more stable ground, ready to work through the difficulties caused by past wounds and begin on the more pleasurable path ahead.

Pleasure Point:

Go to a place where you, as a couple, feel close to God. It may be a mountaintop, the ocean or a lake, the woods, a prayer chapel or church. As a couple, begin your recovery by praying and asking God to heal your hurts.

You may want to use this sample prayer below, compiled from Scripture. You can both pray silently or aloud.

"Lord, you alone can heal us. We let you have all our worries and cares, for you are always thinking about us and watching everything that concerns us. We do not lean on our own understanding. In all our ways we acknowledge you, and you will make our paths straight. You heal the brokenhearted and bind up our wounds. We cry out to you, Lord, in our trouble; save us out of our distresses."[6]

12

THE
PLEASURE
OF PURE
LOVE

WE HOPE THAT BY THIS POINT IN the book you have found some practical steps to take for the kind of marriage you desire. We also realize you may be struggling, wondering if you can really *do* what it takes to achieve that goal. Don't sweat it. The question is common and can help you grow. Wrestling through issues such as these often brings brand new perspectives that lead to healthier marriages.

I (Bill) will never forget the process of deciding to get married. I was convinced that long-term relationships could not sustain happiness, let alone intimate pleasure. Starting a relationship was fun, but it seemed that after a very short time things grew dull.

As I looked around at couples who had been married for a long time, I lost hope. My parents were committed to each other but I was disappointed by the lack of intimacy and passion in their relationship. My friends' parents didn't seem any more in love than my parents were. As I got closer to the age where I was considering marriage, many of my friends' parents were getting divorced and I nearly concluded that a fulfilling marriage was impossible.

My response was to quit dating, thinking, *there must be more important things in life than girls.* I poured my attention into school and ministry among college students.

Then I met Pam. We were at a ministry training conference. On the first night, I asked her if she would go on a date later in the conference. My heart raced as I asked her out. That night I couldn't concentrate on the conference. I had trouble sleeping and couldn't remember anything that was said at the conference the next day.

I didn't know what was happening to me, but it was wonderful—and frightening. I knew I had met a woman who was appealing to me in every way. She had the body type I found attractive, her personality was captivating, her spiritual life was running parallel to my own, and her outlook on life was very similar to mine. I felt as if I could fall in love with this woman, but I was nagged by thoughts that intimate relationships don't stay intimate.

As the relationship progressed, I could see Pam's confidence in our relationship growing. It seemed to me that she was growing in her belief that we would get married. The more she thought about it, the more she liked the idea. On the other hand, I was unwilling to think about the possibility of marriage because I was afraid it would ruin an otherwise good relationship.

It was a confusing time for me. I was growing in my love and desire for Pam but I was afraid to admit it. I was running away from my longing to be married because I was still convinced it could not really work. Then Pam made me face my fears.

In the summer of 1979, Pam was going to Colorado for two months. Before she left she made the following statement:

"Bill, you know I'm going to be gone for two months. We have both been hurt by previous relationships, so we've tried to protect each other's emotions. I think this summer we should not write or call each other, but we should spend the time praying and asking God if we should get married. That way we won't play games with each other. We will either get married or we will break up—either way we will get on with our lives without unnecessary complications. What do you think?"

What do I think? She could not have asked me a more difficult question. I loved her but I felt this would be the end of our relationship.

In June, Pam and I said goodby to each other for the two months. The two-hour drive home from Bakersfield to Thousand Oaks was the longest drive of my life as I had an emotional wrestling match with God.

The battle went something like this.

"God, I'm too young to get married. If I go ahead with this, I will be throwing away my goals. I will be giving up everything I want to accomplish in life. Besides, I can't afford to get married. This is just too big a risk!"

As long as I stayed with that kind of thinking I would get a sick feeling in my stomach. It felt as if someone were chasing me as I frantically tried to escape.

This feeling would get very heavy, so I'd give in and tell God, "All right, God, you can have it your way. I'll marry Pam."

As soon as I would pray this way, a feeling of peace would sweep over me—I felt like a scared child running into the arms of a loving parent. I enjoyed the peace, but after a few minutes I would think about what I was doing and the fear would return. Then I would start arguing with God all over again.

After two hours of going back and forth between peace and turmoil, I finally resigned myself to the fact that God wanted me to marry this woman. I wasn't sure how long we'd be happy, but I figured at least we would have a few good years together.

To my surprise, the pleasure and satisfaction of our marriage has remained and grown over these fourteen years. I have actually gone from believing it couldn't work to believing that anyone who wants a good marriage can have one.

I feel that our relationship has been protected from what I feared by a series of guidelines we have tried to live by. These six principles have also made a pleasurable difference in the marriages of those we have counseled.

1. I will live a balanced life. Life is multidimensional. We are made up of body, soul and spirit. If we are to develop a truly pleasurable life, we must have these in balance.

For example, our body is spoken of as a temple in which God lives.[1] As such, we are encouraged to recognize our body as a valuable asset and not to abuse it in any way.

Regarding the soul, we are encouraged to develop personal disciplines that lead to healthier living. The value of laughter, good friends, honesty, integrity, personal goals and hard work mixed with times of relaxation are all soul-builders.

Spiritual development is vital for strong marriages. Couples who integrate a vibrant spiritual life into the fabric of their relationship will experience more life pleasure than those who operate only in two of the three dimensions of life.

2. I will build trust in our relationship. It is a well-documented truth that trust is a vital element of a marriage.[2] It is especially important in the intimate areas of life. I (Bill) have become aware that if Pam does not trust me she will have a difficult time respecting me.

When I was trying to finish my bachelor's degree, we were without a car. I was riding my bike to school while Pam rode her bike to work. I had a freelance job but was making far less money than Pam. I had an intense struggle trying to feel worthy of Pam's respect. I felt as if I were dragging Pam through the mud as I plowed on to reach my goals.

We had some rough times sorting through who should be making the decisions about money and time commitments. But through it all, Pam continued to trust me and believe that I would succeed. Not even phone calls from friends or relatives questioning the wisdom of my being in school when we didn't even have a car disrupted her resolve to believe in me.

I have learned that when Pam expresses trust in me, I feel I can conquer the world.

A husband who does not trust his wife will have a difficult time sharing his feelings with her. It would be hard to even talk with her, let alone have meaningful sex with her.

A wife who cannot trust her husband will close off areas of her life one by one until she has shut all the doors to her heart. No hurt can get to her, but neither can any love from her husband. Because her heart is sealed off, she cannot let go during lovemaking. It isn't "love"-making anymore. Sex becomes a duty. She may quietly cry herself to sleep at first, but after years of emotional isolation, even the tears will stop.

However, a woman who can completely trust her husband will be amazed at her ability to experience ecstasy during sex. Sometimes my (Pam) intense feelings of desire for Bill surprise me. After fourteen years, my blood still rushes as I drive into the garage after a day away from Bill.

Trust has been built, layer upon layer, in our marriage. The first layer was laid during our dating days as Bill and I discussed the physical standards we wanted for our relationship. Because of prior dating experiences we knew we were both wired hot. We valued the virginity we both held and didn't want an escalating physical relationship to steal that gift away in the heat of a moment. So we set up specific parameters until we were married.

Early in marriage, trust was built up as Bill would first ask, then seek to meet my sexual desires. Trust was also built as he cheered me on to goals that were special to me. I have found that I can give Bill the benefit of the doubt in little things because he is careful to pay attention to the biggest needs in my life. As Bill listened with his heart, my trust in him grew.

Trust has rewarded Bill with a wife who has grown more expressive, adventurous and assertive in her love toward him. Bill's trustworthy character has become his ally in bed. I want to love him the way he wants to be loved because I trust him with my heart.

The Christian life is one of trust. As the four of us have practiced trusting God, we have each learned to trust our spouse. Learning to trust our Maker helps remove the fear of entrusting ourselves to another individual. We can trust him or her, as well as God, with the secrets of our most private selves.

We will never naturally be good at trusting others. Trust is a skill we learn as we walk the path of life. A life in fellowship with God encourages us to practice this ability.

3. I will be there for you. One of the very basic principles of marriage is commitment. You and your spouse are both imperfect people. Your unique backgrounds and childhood baggage can bring conflict into your marriage. If you allow your relationship to be defined by your differences, you will most likely divorce. If, on the other hand, you commit unreservedly to one another, you stand a good chance of working through your differences to a satisfying marriage.

We (Jim and Sally) surveyed 186 couples for our book *Traits of a Lasting Marriage.* The number one factor in marriage longevity was the *resolve* to stay committed, to stay in the marriage and make the marriage a high priority.[3]

Studies have clearly shown that marital success is linked strongly to religious attitudes and behavior. The more active a couple is in a church, the less likely they are to divorce.[4] When commitment is unattractive to us, or we just don't think we have what it takes to carry on, belonging to a community of people who share the same spiritual outlook on life can be invaluable. We have known many people who have found the strength to push through the difficult times of marriage because they knew their friends were cheering them on, praying for them, ready to put an arm around them when necessary. They, in essence, borrowed their friends' belief in marriage when they didn't have the strength to stay committed on their own.

The more committed a couple is to God, the more likely they are to find increasing pleasure in life. Research shows the very interesting fact that women who are strongly religious seem to be more sexually responsive. The religious woman "is more likely than the nonreligious women to be orgasmic almost every time she engages in sex."[5] Tim and Beverly LaHaye surveyed over 3,000 couples and found that 87 percent of men and 85 percent of women who prayed together more than once a week rated their sex life as very good.[6]

I (Pam) was discussing this topic with a friend who had previously lived with the man who was now her husband. She raved about the change that had entered their marriage since they had decided to include God in their personal lives and in their marriage. She smiled as she stated, "I'm much more secure now. I'm not having sex to make sure he stays one more night. I can really relax now that there's a real commitment. Each time we have sex it just gets better and better for me. Now I'm relaxed in his love."

4. I will grow toward my individual best. Personal growth in marriage is both terrific and treacherous. One spouse may be threatened because the mate becomes a different person from the one who walked down the aisle. This can be very disconcerting to the individual who wants to maintain the status quo. It can be just as hard for the person who feels the pressure to grow but is married to someone who stifles that growth.

Pam and I hit a roadblock in this area during our twelfth year of marriage. After the birth of our third child, Pam began to feel a need to plan her future. Being a talented, motivated individual, she recognized she would not be a stay-at-home mom her whole life. If she wanted to have future success in her career, she needed to get more education. She shared her dreams about the future with great enthusiasm. I, on the other hand, reacted with anger and resistance.

I felt as if she were cramping *my* life in order to follow *her* dreams. I felt my desires and my opinion didn't count. I had thought I was a pretty secure man, but I have to admit now that Pam's drive threatened me. I thought if I let Pam run with her dreams, I would have to give up mine, and I wasn't ready to do that.

I will never forget the day I talked with Jim over lunch. I asked him if he had any advice for me on how I could control Pam's schedule so that our life would stay balanced.

I thought I was being very sensitive in trying to keep my priorities straight and support Pam as much as I could. I was stunned when Jim asked, "Do you feel a need to control Pam?"

Immediately I grew defensive. I felt as if I had just been caught lying. I was speechless. Then I stammered and tripped over my thoughts as I tried to come up with a way to justify myself in the face of that well-aimed word of conviction. I was relieved when Jim resumed the conversation about how to balance busy lives.

Jim helped me realize that the Bible places a high premium on personal growth. In fact, when couples expect to grow throughout their marriage, they discover a sense of happy anticipation of their future possibilities. Jim assured me that Pam wasn't out of control but was responding naturally to life's changes. By working with her instead of competing or controlling, I could help us achieve a win-win situation.

5. *I will sacrifice for you.* The paradox in marriage is that *we get by giving.* The more we invest in our relationship the more we receive from it. When we sacrifice for our spouse, our relationship becomes more valuable and the bond is strengthened. Without sacrifice, the marriage is governed by selfish desires and soon disintegrates.

Marriage is a mirror of Christ's compassionate act of death on the cross for our redemption. Husbands are to sacrificially love their wives and meet their needs. In the same way, wives are to sacrificially love their husbands and meet their needs.[7] The end result is that both get their needs met while the relationship is strengthened.

Pam and I have learned much about the benefits of sacrifice in marriage because we have been privileged to be a part of Jim and Sally's life. It is moving to listen to Jim recount how Sally stood by him through a tough mid-life transition, often sacrificing personal needs to meet the needs of a husband with a broken heart. A strong, sensitive woman making sacrifices brings a deeper love to a marriage.

Then to hear the loving way Jim tenderly cared for Sally through her illness with breast cancer has brought tears to our eyes. Jim is an example of a strong, compassionate man whose sacrifice has brought a deeper love to an already strong marriage.

6. *I will honor and respect you.* No one likes to be treated with anything but respect. The feminist movement has been a response to the lack of respect women have experienced at the hands of men. The soaring divorce rate in America has been fueled by the lack of esteem that has become rampant. To have a truly intimate and happy marriage, mutual respect between a husband and wife is crucial.

To this end, a mutual relationship is extremely beneficial. The Bible clearly teaches that we are all equal. As a result, all individuals have the same value and are worthy of the same honor. The Bible has us practice "preferring one another in honor," "considering one another as more important than yourself." An individual who is trained to show honor even to those to whom he is not intimately related will be more likely to respect the one he loves.

It has not always been a breeze to choose to express respect to Bill. After he served as a youth pastor at a church in Bakersfield for four years, we moved to San Diego. We were both excited to see Bill pastor his first church. But my excitement soon turned to sadness. In our first few months in San Diego, I fought the worst depression of my life. I was missing close friends, our first home and the comfortable, growing ministry we had shared in Bakersfield. I felt alone in my struggle to find where I would fit in this new city.

I started to entertain negative thoughts like "Bill doesn't care. He's so busy doing what he's always wanted to do that he's not even noticing my pain." I began to lash out at Bill, treating him with anger and contempt at times when I had previously expressed trust and respect.

One day, I went to my closet to get something and started crying. I sat down on the floor and cried out to God, saying, "I'm not going to talk to anyone about this except you. I know Bill deserves my honor and respect. He's earned my trust. God, I will spend time in your Word until you give me an answer to my pain. I need to honor Bill—but you have to give me the ability."

I opened my Bible and read a very familiar verse, yet it spoke volumes to my heart that day. It was simply a few words: "a wife must *respect* her husband."[8]

I got out a dictionary and a thesaurus and read all the synonyms for respect. I came up with three ways to show respect to Bill. First, I would see Bill as God saw him (instead of with my distorted view from my depression). Second, I would talk to Bill as

God would (I would speak kindly and clearly, valuing him as a person). Third, I would treat Bill as God would (loving him unconditionally, sacrificing for his good).

The next day I showed up at Bill's office and asked if I could take him to lunch. I told him I was sorry he had taken the brunt of my sadness, explained to him my story and what I was resolving to do. I then held his hands, looked into his eyes and told him, "Regardless of what happens, whether or not I get the things that I think will make me happy, please know that from this moment on I am on your team. I believe in you. I love you."

The circumstances of the move and the broken dreams I blamed for my depression didn't change right away, but my attitude did. I was freed from the dark clouds that had separated me from the one I love. I gave my respect and my heart back to Bill.

There was an immediate change in Bill. A huge burden seemed to lift off his shoulders.

I learned that when Bill receives respect from me, he feels a sense of confidence that leads him to increased productivity and a heightened sense of his own worth. Under these conditions, he considers it a privilege to be married to a wife who is supportive.

However, a man who feels his wife does not respect him gets frustrated and angry as he struggles with his own sense of worth. This man is often demotivated and buries his real feelings. He frequently shifts his energies and insights away from his marriage to his career.

A woman who feels respected by her husband has a sense of confidence and an increased sense of security. From this secure position, the wife is willing to share of herself to see that her husband's needs are met and mutual goals are accomplished.

A woman who does not feel respect from her husband will struggle with a declining self-image and a dwindling confidence in her ability to be a wife, a lover—or a person.

Empowered
The ability to say and live out these six principles comes by the power of God enabling each of our lives. But the question remains, "How do we get this special power from God into our marriage?"

Launching this powerful relationship with God can be compared to the commitment between two people at marriage. A couple commits to each other their:
☐ love
☐ future
☐ past
☐ faithfulness
☐ bodies
☐ wealth

In short, each person gives all he or she has been, is currently, and ever hopes to be, to the other person. They each relinquish their total control over their destiny and invite the other to mold, share and be a full participant in all of their life.

It is exactly the same in our relationship with God. We give all our being to God and invite him to be a full participant in our lives. This commitment of our whole being to God then allows him the freedom to empower us to be greater in our love for our mate than would have been possible without his supernatural love.

A pleasurable marriage for us (Farrels and Conways) did not begin on the day we met our mate, or on the day of our wedding, but on the day we each met Jesus personally. As we live out our marriage under the lordship of Christ, "Pure Pleasure" is becoming a reality, moment by moment, day by day, year by year.

Pleasure Point:
After the two of you have been together sexually, while you are still

holding each other, express one of the statements of love from this chapter in your own words, then pray for each other, thanking God for his love and care.

To continue deepening your marital pleasure, read God's promises listed below. Then renew your commitment to follow God with your whole heart, with your mate as your witness.

God's Statement of Love to Us

☐ I love you and have a plan for you.

"I came to give life—life in all its fullness." (John 10:10)

"I came so they can have real and eternal life, more and better life than they ever dreamed of." (John 10:10, *The Message*)

"For God loved the world so much that he gave his only Son so that whoever believes in him may not be lost, but have eternal life." (John 3:16)

☐ I know you are imperfect so you are separated from my love; our relationship is broken.

"All people have sinned and are not good enough for God's glory." (Romans 3:23)

"We've compiled this long and sorry record as sinners . . . and proved that we are utterly incapable of living the glorious lives God wills for us." (Romans 3:23, *The Message*)

"And when a person knows the right thing to do but does not do it, then he is sinning." (James 4:17)

"It is your evil that has separated you from your God. Your sins cause him to turn away from you." (Isaiah 59:2)

☐ I love you, so I, who am perfect, paid the price for your imperfection so I could restore our relationship.

"But Christ died for us while we were still sinners. In this way God shows his great love for us. We have been made right with God by the blood of Christ's death. So through Christ we will surely be saved from God's anger. I mean that while we were God's enemies, God made friends with us through the death of his Son. Surely, now we are God's friends. God will save us through his Son's life." (Romans 5:8-10)

"Christ had no sin. But God made him become sin. God did this for us so that in Christ we could become right with God." (2 Corinthians 5:21)

"Christ himself died for you. And that one death paid for your sins. He was not guilty, but he died for those who are guilty. He did this to bring you all to God." (1 Peter 3:18)

"The greatest love a person can show is to die for his friends." (John 15:13)

☐ To initiate this new relationship, all you need to do is to accept my payment for your imperfection. I cannot make you love me; that is your choice.

"I mean that you have been saved by grace because you believe you did not save yourselves. It was a gift from God. You cannot brag that you are saved by the work you have done. God has made us what we are. In Christ Jesus, God made us new people." (Ephesians 2:8-10)

"If you use your mouth to say 'Jesus is Lord' and if you believe in your heart God raised Jesus from death, then you will be saved." (Romans 10:9)

"And this is eternal life: that men can know you, the only true God, and that men can know Jesus Christ, the One you sent." (John 17:3)[9] To accept God's love for you, talk to him; let him lead the decision-making part of your life. This is a sample prayer:

Jesus, I am sorry I have chosen to live apart from you. I want you in my life. I accept the payment of love you gave for me by your death on the cross. Thank you for being my best friend and my God.

Appendix A: Activities to Deepen Your Pleasure

Chapter One: Longing for Pleasure

Which picture best describes how you see God as he looks at your life:

    God is crying

    God is like a lightning bolt

    God has his back to me

    God is carrying me

    God is smiling

    God is laughing

    God isn't there

    God is giving a standing ovation

Why did you choose that answer? Share your thoughts with your spouse.

Chapter Two: The Pleasure of Commitment

Decision-making can be life-altering. Because of this, some decisions can seem overwhelming. The Bible clearly teaches that God wants to be a part of our decisions. "But if any of you lacks wisdom, let him ask of God, who gives to all men generously, and without reproach, and it will be given to him."[1]

All through this book, you will be making decisions; therefore, the four of us recommend that you invite God into this process.

Choose one of the action points below to do as a couple to express this attitude of including God.

☐ Pray together a simple prayer, at a meal or in bed at night, such as, "God, we want you to be a part of our marriage. Please help us with all our decisions. Amen."

☐ Make a card to stick on your refrigerator or mirror that says, "What's God's opinion?"

☐ Go to a Christian bookstore and buy either *Strong's Exhaustive Concordance* or *Nave's Topical Bible* so you can look up verses by topic or key words to learn what God says on a particular subject. After locating the verse reference, you can turn to the front of your Bible and locate the page numbers for each book. Some Bible translations you may enjoy are: New International Version, New King James Version, New American Standard Version, Living Bible and New Century Version.

Chapter Three: The Pleasure of Being Understood

The Bible says, "Let no unwholesome word proceed from your mouth, but only such a word as is good for edification according to the need of the moment that it may give grace to those who hear."[2]

Ask your mate to list the two or three phrases you use most often that hurt or irritate. Ask him or her to try to reword it for you in a way that would be more positive to hear. Some examples:

Pam says: "Bill, you NEED to do . . ."

Bill rewords: "Bill, I have an idea I'd like to run by you."

Jim says: "Sally, you always interrupt me when I am talking."

Sally rewords: "Sally, I know I often pause when I'm talking. Could you wait while I gather my thoughts?"

Chapter Four: The Pleasure of Love Under Pressure

Over a quiet lunch or dinner, discuss these questions:

Which of these six statements would you like to have read at your 50th wedding anniversary party? Why?

☐ We listen with our hearts

☐ We love each other passionately

☐ We are kind, gentle and attentive—best friends

☐ We are having a really fun life

☐ We bring out the best in each other

☐ We love each other in a way that mirrors God's love for the world

The Bible says "Teach us to number our days . . . that we may gain a heart of wisdom."[3] What are some wise changes you could make in the next few years that could help insure that your chosen statement would be true at your 50th anniversary?

Chapter Five: The Pleasure of Forgiveness

Forgiveness is sometimes very difficult. To help you verbalize your complete forgiveness, it is good to personalize God's Word, the Bible, to your own life. Jesus is a personal Savior for each one of us. Absolutely nothing is impossible for him to forgive; that's why he died on the cross.

If you have received Jesus Christ into your life, his Holy Spirit resides in you. Because of that relationship, you can choose to forgive another through Christ's power in you. Rather than relying on your own ability, you can lean on his infinitely abundant power to forgive—even if you feel the person doesn't deserve forgiveness. This is where healing and lasting love begin.

Take turns reading the following verses aloud, first inserting your own name—choosing to forgive yourself. Then repeat and insert your mate's name—choosing to extend forgiveness to him or her.

_____ [has died on the cross] with Christ and it is no longer _____ who lives, but Christ lives in _____ ;

and the life which _____ now lives in the flesh, _____ lives by faith in the Son of God, who loved _____ and delivered himself up for _____ . Therefore if _____ is in Christ, _____ is a new creature; the old things passed away; behold new things have come.

I will be kind to you, _____, tenderhearted, forgiving you just as God in Christ also has forgiven me.[4]

Chapter Six: The Pleasure of Faithfulness

Women have affairs because they feel estranged from their husbands. Men have affairs due to physical or emotional attraction or marital dissatisfaction. Think about a time you felt vulnerable to an affair (or had one). What one thing could you do now, and what one thing could your mate do for you, to safeguard your relationship? Share your ideas with each other.

God promises to give you a way out when tempted.[5] Look for it now! Ask your spouse these questions to see if there are any temptations on the horizon:

1. Do I compliment members of the opposite sex based more on their value than on appearance? Am I complimenting any one person too often in a way that he or she might misinterpret my comments?

2. Am I spending enough time with you?

3. Am I spending too much alone time with someone other than you? Am I protecting my reputation from any unwarranted speculation? Are there innocent things I do that could lead you or someone else to think I am unfaithful?

4. Am I touching someone of the opposite sex in a way that makes you uncomfortable, or is someone touching me in a way that makes you uncomfortable?

5. Am I talking about someone in a way that makes you uncomfortable?

Chapter Seven: The Pleasure of Authentic Desire

God offers some great sexual advice.[6] God recommends that the marriage bed be undefiled.[7] That simply means it is only for you two. Because God places such a high priority on the symbol of the marriage bed, what one improvement could you make to your room or your bed that would symbolize the priority of the marriage bed to you as a couple?

For example, in our first year of marriage we (Bill and Pam) made a promise to each other not to pile stuff on the bed so it would be ready to use whenever we desired. On our tenth anniversary, we splurged for a new bed, headboard, mattress and bedding as a reward for ten great years and a way to say we look forward to our next ten years in bed!

Chapter Eight: The Pleasure of Self-Control

The Bible says, "Finally, brethren, whatever is true, whatever is honorable, whatever is right, whatever is pure, whatever is lovely, whatever is of good repute, if there is any excellence and if anything worthy of praise, let your mind dwell on these things."[8]

Using the key words of the above verse, each of you make a list of romantic or sexual activities that come to your mind after each word listed below. Share your lists and discuss the similarities and differences.

True

Example: Your body is perfect for me. I especially love your breasts when I . . .

Honorable

Example: Sex with you and no one else.

Right

Example: When you are thoughtful—like when I have to go out of town and you pack notes of encouragement in my suitcase and have a new nightie waiting when I get home. I like to know you've missed me.

Pure
   Example: Standing in front of French doors at a beach house
   in a crisp white sundress, with my tanned husband kissing my
   neck and his arms around me.
Lovely
   Example: Long-stemmed roses, classical music, tea by a fire,
   white linen on the table, a seafood dinner and sparkling grape
   juice in chilled crystal glasses.
Of Good Repute
   Example: Keeping our special sexual times private. I like it to
   be a secret between just us two.
Excellent
   Example: The songs you write for me.
Worthy of Praise
   Example: Your hair in the sunlight. The way you spontaneously
   give while lovemaking. The way you express your desire for
   me—that gives me confidence.

Chapter Nine: The Pleasure of Passion

Read the Song of Songs aloud as a couple every day for a week.
Take turns reading the parts; for example, the wife could read all
the bride's verses and the husband all of Solomon's. Call your
spouse on the phone and read a section, or copy a few verses and
slip them in a lunchbox, card or briefcase.

Chapter Ten: The Pleasure of Fun

The Bible clearly teaches that God is the author of joy.[9] Choose
one of these creative ways to get to know the God of joy better.
   ☐ Go to a Christian bookstore and rent a video on marriage, then
make popcorn and watch the video together.
   ☐ Buy one of the books recommended in *Pure Pleasure* and
read a chapter a week together on your date night.
   ☐ Go to a Christian music concert or drama production, or at-

tend a service at a church which treats the Bible seriously.

☐ Buy romantic music that builds your marriage. Favorite artists of the four of us are Steve and Annie Chapman, who write and sing great marriage songs.[10]

☐ Go for a walk in nature. Stop a moment and take turns praying to God, thanking him for all of his creation, especially your mate, who has specific qualities you enjoy.

Chapter Eleven: The Pleasure of Decisiveness

Emotional wounds in a marriage can be extremely stressful and difficult to work through. It is at these times that outside support can lift some of the stress off the marriage. Each of you may want to choose one or two trusted friends (or a counselor or pastor) to work with you in your healing process. These friends need to commit to:

☐ Meet regularly for prayer and accountability
☐ Be available in case of crisis
☐ Encourage you
☐ Maintain confidentiality

Chapter Twelve: The Pleasure of Pure Love

Investing in your marriage is a necessary priority for all married couples. A Hebrew word used to describe marriage, *qedûshîm*, means "consecration." It is the same word used in the Old Testament to describe the utensils that were used in the offering of sacrifices in the temple. The implication was that all these utensils were part of God's house and belonged to God. The implication for marriage today is that your marriage is the personal possession of God. Since God owns your marriage and considers it a very valuable possession, he invests in it.

The four of us have been the recipients of some excellent teaching and counsel in this area. But we purposefully plan times each year to build our own marriages. Many seminars, retreats and conferences are available to help build your marriage. A few that we have seen as profitable are:

Christian Marriage Enrichment (with Norm Wright)
1913 East 17th St., Suite 118
Santa Ana, CA 92701
(714) 542-3506

Christian Marriage Encounter
(800) 795-5683 for an information packet

Marriage Tune-Up (with John and Jacque Coulombe)
(714) 529-5544

Today's Family (with John Trent and Gary Smalley)
(417) 335-4321 to find a conference near you

Family Life Today (with Dennis and Barbara Rainey)
P.O. Box 23840
Little Rock, AR 72221
(800) 333-1433

We are also available for conferences:

Jim and Sally Conway
Mid-Life Dimensions
P.O. Box 3790
Fullerton, CA 92634

Bill and Pam Farrel
Masterful Living
629 S. Rancho Santa Fe Rd., #306
San Marcos, CA 92069

Appendix B: Resources for Recapturing Pleasure

The emotional fallout of the sexual revolution has only begun to be felt. The helping professions are inundated with people in search of recovery. Those wounded by the sexual revolution often require special in-depth help for specific problems. This help can come from a good self-help book on the topic, a support group or Bible study group that addresses the particular need, or professional counseling from a trained pastor or psychotherapist.

Below are some helpful resources to aid victims in regaining wholeness and discovering the pleasure and passion of which the sexual revolution may have robbed them.

Abortion Recovery

Sarah sat cross-legged on the floor folding laundry. She had a box of tissue in her lap.

"I miss my baby. No one told me that if I got an abortion it would be so painful ten years later. I know I should be grateful for the two kids I have, but I wonder what their big brother or sister would have been like. Sometimes I just break into tears when I see a kid who is the same age my child would have been. They told me it was just a lump of tissue. It doesn't feel like tissue to me. It feels like a real baby—my baby. One that I'll never hold."

Sarah is just one of many woman who experience post-abortion trauma. Most prolife organizations have a wing that reaches out to women who are experiencing post-abortion trauma. There are also special groups that specialize in this area. One group, *Silent Voices,* has helped many women gain the healing they long for. Symptoms of post-abortion syndrome can include:

Physical symptoms:
   Infertility or difficulty conceiving
   Sterility
   Stillbirths
   Premature births
   Miscarriages
   Tubal/ectopic pregnancies
   Pelvic Inflammatory Disease
   Abdominal pain

Emotional symptoms:
   Sexual dysfunction
   Guilt
   Suicidal impulses
   Drug/alcohol abuse
   Despair/helplessness
   Regret/remorse
   Desire to get pregnant again
   Low self-esteem
   Crying unexpectedly or uncontrollably
   Frigidity
   Anorexia/bulimia
   Preoccupation with death
   Preoccupation with the aborted baby

Nightmares concerning babies
Inability to make decisions
Need to control situations[1]

A woman commonly disconnects from relationships to handle her emotional stress by using a handful of defense mechanisms:

She may *suppress* emotions by acknowledging the abortion while she walls off any feelings she might have about it.

She may *repress* her feelings by trying to "forget" that it ever happened.

She may *rationalize* her feelings by explaining away why she had the abortion, trying to make an intolerable situation tolerable by self-deceiving mind games.

She may *deny* her feelings and actually say, even believe, that she never had an abortion.

She may *compensate* by having another baby. Eighty-five percent of all women have another pregnancy within a year of an abortion.[2]

She may also become a *supermom* to future children, striving to make up for her loss of the aborted child.

She may also feel *unable to bond* with her new babies because she has sealed off her feelings because of the abortion.

It has been our experience that most women who experience an abortion have a delayed reaction to its effects. Often the above symptoms become the camouflage right after the abortion, providing a feeling of relief, as if a problem has been solved. However, several years later, often during the childbearing years of marriage, the sense of loss, guilt and maternal longings reappear.

Those who have had the most success recovering from the ill effects of an abortion are those who confront the problem head on. They admit an abortion was not a positive solution to the problem. Counseling and support groups also speed recovery. Recuperation is also aided by helping other women who have been similarly wounded.

For information about post-abortion syndrome contact these sources:

Silent Voices
191 Glover Avenue, Suite B
Chula Vista, CA 91910
(619) 422-0757

National Post-Abortion Reconciliation and Healing Helpline
(800) 5WE-CARE

Reardon, David. *Aborted Women Silent No More.* Westchester, Ill.: Crossway Books, 1987.

Pornography/Sexual Addiction

If you are concerned that you may have a sexual addiction, ask yourself these questions:

1. Are your sexual thoughts and behaviors causing problems in your life?

2. Have your sexual thoughts and behaviors interfered with your ability to function at home, work or school?

3. Do you fail to meet commitments or carry out responsibilities due to your sexual behaviors or thoughts?

4. Do you struggle to control or stop sexual thoughts and behaviors only to find that you fail time and time again?

5. Do you spend money on sexual activities or sexual material?

6. Do you feel guilty or shameful after engaging in sexual activity or sexual fantasy?

7. Do you risk danger by not taking reasonable precautions or by going to unsafe places in order to have sex?

8. Has an important relationship ended because of your inability to curtail sexual activities in or outside of that relationship?

9. Do you undress, masturbate or engage in other sexual ac-

tivities in places where you are likely to be seen by strangers?

10. Have you ever been arrested as a result of your sexual activities or behaviors?

11. Has your pursuit of sexual activity become more compulsive and ritualized?

12. Do you resort to sex to escape, relieve anxiety or just cope with problems?[3]

A yes answer to any of these questions may indicate a sexual addiction. You should seek further help.

We are especially grateful to Aaron J. Reinicke, M.S., for his help in compiling information and resources in this area. He is a licensed marriage, family and child therapist. He is available to speak on this subject and can be reached at:

Reinicke Institute
3430 Camino del Rio North, Suite 200
San Diego, CA 92108
(619) 584-4920

Other helpful resources:

Sexaholics Anonymous
P.O. Box 300
Simi Valley, CA 93062

Sex Addicts Anonymous
P.O. Box 3038
Minneapolis, MN 55403

Sex and Love Addicts Anonymous
P.O. Box 529
Newton, MA 02158

National Council on Sexual Addiction and Compulsivity
P.O. Box 64657
Tucson, AZ 85728
(800) 321-2066

(213) 546-3101 in CA
(800) 622-9494 outside CA

Del Amo Hospital Helpline
(800) 551-9888

Tapes: Desert Streams Tapes
1415 Santa Monica Mall, #201
Santa Monica, CA 90401

Newsletter: Tracks in the Sand (for men)
P.O. Box 1828
Tustin, CA 92680
(714) 751-1012

Books:
Caton, David. *Overcoming the Addiction to Pornography.* Amer-
     ican Family Association, P.O. Box 82722, Tampa, FL 33682.
     $9.45. Orders are confidential.
Dalby, Gordon. *Healing of the Masculine Soul.* Dallas, Tex.: Word,
     1988.
Friends in Recovery Staff. *The Twelve Steps: A Spiritual Journey.*
     San Diego, Calif.: Friends in Recovery, 1988.
Joy, Donald. *Unfinished Business.* Wheaton, Ill.: Victor Books,
     1989.
Anonymous. "The War Within: An Anatomy of Lust." *Leadership
     Journal,* Fall 1982, pp. 30-46.

Sexual Abuse

By far, this is the greatest area of prolonged woundedness the counseling community has seen. Current estimates show that up to 31 percent of females report being sexually abused as a child, and 16 percent of males report this same trauma. One study found that if the researcher asked specific questions about experiences of a sexual nature in childhood, the results grew to 55 percent of all women having an inappropriate sexual contact while growing up. The sexual parameters have been so eschewed that victims are even rationalizing their perpetrators' behavior.[4]

Every one of these types of abuse is devastating because every number represents a person. A person with a story. A person who may have children. The cycle continues as these children have a story of their own and, now that they are married, they are wondering if this same story will be passed on to their children.

It is common for men and women to totally block out memories of abuse for years. Often memories erupt when they are married or begin to parent. Most people need professional help in dealing with this delicate and painful area of woundedness.

Some helpful reading:

Frank, Don and Jan. *When Victims Marry.* San Bernardino, Calif.: Here's Life Publishers, 1990.

Frank, Jan. *A Door of Hope.* San Bernardino, Calif.: Here's Life Publishers, 1987.

Seamands, David. *Healing for Damaged Emotions.* Wheaton, Ill.: Victor Books, 1887.

———. *The Healing of Memories.* Wheaton, Ill.: Victor Books, 1985.

Affairs

Swift action is very important if you suspect your spouse is having an adulterous affair. It is crucial to know from day one how to handle your emotions and the actions of your mate. To maximize the chances of saving a marriage, get wise counsel and read.

Conway, Jim. *Men in Mid-Life Crisis.* Elgin, Ill.: David C. Cook, 1978.
Conway, Jim and Sally. *When a Mate Wants Out.* Grand Rapids, Mich.: Zondervan, 1992.
Jenkins, Jerry. *Loving Your Marriage Enough to Protect It.* Chicago: Moody, 1989.
Peterson, J. Allen. *The Myth of the Greener Grass.* Wheaton, Ill.: Tyndale House, 1991.

Divorce
Those who are newly divorced are very susceptible to "rebound" relationships. The authors of the *Fresh Start Recovery Workbook* warn those hurting from divorce that it may take three to five years to rebuild trust. Those who experience divorce should "go back to your original divorce and work through those issues. If you don't, you're just going to take the same issues into the next relationship and the next. You've got to stop, put your heart in a cast, and go back and work on the original issues."[5]

Fresh Start Ministries
63 Chestnut Road
Paoli, PA 19301
(800) 882-2799 in Pennsylvania
(215) 644-6464 outside Pennsylvania

If your parents divorced, you may still be affected now as an adult. It is important for you to sort through issues and gain perspective and healing. A book that can help is:

Conway, Jim. *Adult Children of Legal or Emotional Divorce.* Downers Grove, Ill.: InterVarsity Press, 1990.

Rape

Rape, too, is at an epidemic level. In one survey, 51 percent of men said they would rape if they thought they could get away with it.[6] Twenty percent of women report that they have been date raped, and authorities in this area estimate that only 5 percent of victims ever report the crime.[7]

The tragedy of rape can be the most misunderstood and confusing crime. If it occurs while a couple is married, immediate individual and couple counseling is imperative. If the rape happened to the woman prior to her marriage, the effects can sometimes be masked, and individual and couple counseling is still a very wise intervention.

Candace Walters, in *Invisible Wounds,* describes a simple three-step process for rape victims:

1. Get safe.
2. Get help.
3. Get care.[8]

It is most confusing to a woman when the perpetrator of the rape is a friend, acquaintance or even fiancé. The woman may react with mistrust toward her marriage partner; she may be haunted by unwarranted guilt; and she may want to avoid some types of sexual intimacy or the sex act altogether.

Because the act was a betrayal of trust and produced feelings of helplessness, many of the steps for recovery from sexual abuse are helpful for women and couples in this circumstance. "You do not have to become one of rape's marred-for-life victims, because you choose your own response."[9] Choose to get help for yourself and your loved ones. These books will be useful:

Scott, Kay. *Sexual Assault: Will I Ever Feel Okay Again?* Minneapolis, Minn.: Bethany House, 1993.

Walters, Candace. *Invisible Wounds*. Portland, Ore.: Multnomah, 1987.

Books on Basic Sexual Questions or Marital Helps

Arp, Dave and Claudia. *52 Dates for You and Your Mate*. Nashville: Thomas Nelson, 1993.

Conway, Jim and Sally. *Traits of a Lasting Marriage*. Rev. ed. Downers Grove, Ill.: InterVarsity Press, 1991.

Dillow, Joseph. *Solomon on Sex*. New York: Thomas Nelson, 1977.

LaHaye, Tim and Beverly. *The Act of Marriage*. Grand Rapids, Mich.: Zondervan, 1976.

Penner, Cliff and Joyce. *The Gift of Sex*. Waco, Tex.: Word, 1981.

———. *Restoring the Pleasure*. Dallas, Tex.: Word, 1993.

Swihart, Judson J. *How Do You Say, "I Love You"?* Downers Grove, Ill.: InterVarsity Press, 1977.

Wheat, Ed and Gaye. *Intended for Pleasure*. Old Tappan, N.J.: Revell, 1977. Tapes are also available by Ed Wheat: "Sex Technique and Sex Problems in Marriage" and "Love Life for Every Married Couple." Order from (800) 643-3477.

Books on Parenting

Since many readers of this book may also be parents, below are a few resources to help you lay out a plan to educate your children on relationship and sexual choices.

Dobson, James C. *Preparing for Adolescence*. Ventura, Calif.: Regal Books, 1989.

LaHaye, Tim. *Sex Education Is for the Family*. Grand Rapids, Mich.: Zondervan, 1985.

McDowell, Josh, and Dick Day. *Why Wait?* San Bernardino, Calif.: Here's Life Publishers, 1987.

Healing for a Variety of Hurts

Overcomers Outreach
2290 W. Whittier Blvd., Suite D
La Habra, CA 90631
(213) 697-3994

National Association for Christian Recovery
P.O. Box 11095
Whittier, CA 90603

Focus on the Family
Colorado Springs, CO 80995
(719) 531-5181 (to order a variety of resources or for referrals to find help for specific needs)

Minirth-Meier
(800) 545-1819
Clinics are available across the country. Call for the one nearest you.

Anderson, Neil. *The Bondage Breaker.* Eugene, Ore.: Harvest House, 1990.
_____ . *Victory over Darkness.* Ventura, Calif.: Regal, 1990.
Arthur, Kay. *Lord, Heal My Hurts.* Portland, Ore.: Multnomah Press, 1988.
Life Recovery Guides: study guides on recovery from bitterness, addictions, shame, family dysfunctions, guilt, workaholism, codependency, abuse and so on. Available from InterVarsity Press, P.O. Box 1400, Downers Grove, IL 60515.

Notes

Introduction

[1]Important facts about the sexual revolution:

1954: Hugh Hefner publishes *Playboy* magazine.

1960: FDA approves "the Pill." Seen as a blessing by married women, it is soon being used by single women as well.

1963: *The Feminine Mystique* by Betty Friedan calls women out of their "comfortable concentration camps." The women's movement is in full swing.

1969: Woodstock. A huge rock concert, seen as a symbolic celebration of the revolution because nudity, drugs and sex were plentiful and open. President Johnson's Commission on Obscenity recommends the abolishment of all pornography laws. (Later, President Reagan's Commission on Pornography would link pornography to violence and sexual crimes and recommend full enforcement of laws.) Sexually explicit theater productions like *Hair* with its nude scene and explicitly themed films like *The Graduate* (sex with mother then daughter) and *Bob and Carol, Ted and Alice* (open marriage). Chappaquiddick incident—a rumored liaison between Senator Ted Kennedy and Mary Jo Kopechne which ended in her death in a mysterious car accident. Gay Power riots in New York's Greenwich Village.

1971: Publication of *Our Bodies, Ourselves.* This volume explored and promoted masturbation, lesbianism, abortion on demand and various free-sex practices. It became a handbook for the women's movement.

1972: *Roe v. Wade* legalizes abortion on demand. Beatniks, flower children, hippies and antiwar free-love movement hit the mainstream and introduce communal living, the drug culture and open marriage. Poets, writers and professors take up the free-love philosophy and promote it along with rock and roll groups like the Who, the Beatles and the Rolling Stones.

[2]Geneva Kilburn Hickman, "Former Teacher Reflects on Changes Since Prayer Was Re-

moved from School," *Good News, Etc.,* October 1992, p. 24.

Chapter 1: Longing for Pleasure

[1]*Jenny Jones Show,* NBC, January 11, 1992.

[2]Ellen Goodman, "Madonna's Artistic Integrity? She Doesn't Know How to Spell It," *Times Advocate,* October 27, 1992, p. A7.

[3]*Dateline,* ABC, November 17, 1992.

[4]Barry L. Sherman and Joseph R. Dominick, "Violence and Sex in Music Videos: TV and Rock 'n' Roll," *Journal of Communication* 36, no. 1 (Winter 1986): 79-93.

[5]Melinda Henneberger and Michel Marriott, "Teens Say Abusing Girls Is Part of Dating Ritual," *Times Advocate,* July 11, 1993, pp. 1, 9.

[6]Ibid. For an in-depth discussion on sexual harassment, see Jim and Sally Conway, *Sexual Harassment No More* (Downers Grove, Ill.: InterVarsity Press, 1993).

[7]Catherine Crocker, "Study: Girls Have More Sex Partners," *Times Advocate,* December 11, 1992, p. A6.

[8]John Marchese, "Why Even Nice Guys Give Mixed Signals," *Mademoiselle,* January 1993, p. 44.

[9]Steven Gibb, *Twentysomething* (Chicago: Noble Press, 1991), p. 33.

[10]Koray Tanfer and Jeannette J. Schoorl, "Premarital Sexual Careers and Partner Change," *Archives of Sexual Behavior* 21, no. 1: 52.

[11]Ibid., p. 64.

[12]Andrew Greeley, Robert Michael and Tom Smith, "Americans and Their Sexual Partners," *Society,* July/August 1990, p. 39.

[13]Tanfer and Schoorl, "Premarital Sexual Careers and Partner Change," p. 57.

[14]Harold Leitenberg, Evan Greenwald and Mathew J. Terran, "Correlation Between Sexual Activity Among Children, Preadolescence and/or Early Adolescence and Behavior and Sexual Adjustment in Adulthood," *Archives of Sexual Behavior* 18, no. 4 (1989): 309.

[15]Leslie Brenner, "The Janus Report: Other People's Sex Lives," *Redbook,* March 1993, p. 114.

[16]Kathleen McKinney and Susan Sprecher, eds., *Sexuality in Close Relationships* (Hillsdale, N.J.: Eribaum Lawrence Associates, 1991), p. 64.

[17]Beth Livermore, "The Lessons of Love," *Psychology Today,* March/April 1993, p. 32.

[18]Roger Hillerstrom, *Intimate Deception* (Portland, Ore.: Multnomah Press, 1989), p. 28.

[19]"Demographics and Divorce," *Times Advocate,* September 19, 1992, p. B2.

[20]George Barna, *The Invisible Generation* (Glendale, Calif.: Barna Group, 1992), p. 145.

[21]Ibid., p. 85.

[22]Frank Haycock and Patricia Garwood, *Hidden Bedroom Partners* (San Diego, Calif.: Libra, 1989), p. 15.

[23]Barna, *The Invisible Generation,* p. 140.

[24]Carole Mayhall, "Happily Married," *Today's Christian Woman,* January 1993, p. 30.

Chapter 2: The Pleasure of Commitment

[1]McKinney and Sprecher, *Sexuality in Close Relationships,* p. 63.

[2]Ibid., p. 41. McKinney and Sprecher note research by Stephan, Berscheid, and Walster (1971) which demonstrated that sexual arousal has been found to lead directly to greater general romantic attraction. They note that Berscheid and Walster (1974) as well as

Dutton and Aaron (1974) interpreted this to mean that "generalized physiological arous-al in the presence of an appropriate object of attraction is misattributed to feeling attraction to the object."

[3]John Roache, "Premarital Sexual Attitudes and Behaviors by Stages," *Adolescence* 21, no. 81 (1986): 119.

[4]Ibid., p. 114.

[5]Ibid., pp. 107-20.

Five categories of dating couples were designated in this study: (1) dating with no particular affection; (2) dating with affection but not love; (3) dating and being in love; (4) dating one person only and being in love; (5) engaged.

The five groups were asked to give responses in eight behavioral categories: (1) no physical contact; (2) good-night kiss; (3) several hugs and kisses; (4) prolonged kissing and hugging; (5) light petting above the waist; (6) heavy petting below the waist; (7) mutual masturbation; (8) sexual intercourse.

The study showed several interesting results: (1) In every category the respondents were more active than they deemed proper. (2) In every category respondents thought others were more active than they were. (3) A majority of male respondents considered all eight behavioral categories as proper when at dating stage 3. (4) A majority of female respondents considered all eight behavioral categories as proper when at dating stage 4. (5) Men overall expected sexual activity sooner in the relationship than women. (6) By dating stage 4, male and female responses to all eight behaviors were statistically the same. (7) Those respondents who considered religion to be important had more con-servative attitudes and behaviors.

[6]Leitenberg, Greenwald and Terran, "Correlation Between Sexual Activity," p. 309.

[7]Ibid., p. 311.

[8]Josh McDowell and Dick Day, *Why Wait?* (San Bernardino, Calif.: Here's Life Publishers, 1987), p. 257.

[9]Tim and Beverly LaHaye, *The Act of Marriage* (Grand Rapids, Mich.: Zondervan, 1976), pp. 211, 223.

[10]Roache, "Premarital Sexual Attitudes," p. 119.

[11]Hillerstrom, *Intimate Deception,* p. 28. Thirty-five percent of those who have cohabited will end marriage before the fifteenth anniversary compared to 19 percent who didn't cohabit.

[12]Ibid., p. 136.

[13]Barna, *The Invisible Generation,* p. 140.

[14]Ibid., p. 32.

[15]*D.O.A.,* Touchstone Pictures, dir. Rocky Morton and Annabel Jankel, screenplay by Charles Pogue, 1988.

Chapter 3: The Pleasure of Being Understood

[1]Helen Fisher, "The Four Year Itch," *USA Weekend,* October 23-25, 1992, p. 5.

[2]Clifford and Joyce Penner, *The Gift of Sex* (Waco, Tex.: Word, 1981), p. 209.

[3]Jim and Sally Conway, *Traits of a Lasting Marriage* (Downers Grove, Ill.: InterVarsity Press, 1991), p. 75.

[4]Ibid., p. 69. We have further explored marriage communication in *When a Mate Wants Out* (Grand Rapids, Mich.: Zondervan, 1992).

[5]Jim Conway, *Making Real Friends in a Phony World* (Grand Rapids, Mich.: Zondervan, 1989). Jim's book covers major communication skills like: 1. Attending: Focusing on Your Friend; 2. Listening: One Part of Communication; 3. Talking: Another Part of Communication; 4. Empathy: Caring Enough to Send Your Very Best; 5. Genuineness: Being Real in a Phony World; 6. Affirmation: Passing On Blessing.

Chapter 4: The Pleasure of Love Under Pressure
[1]Quoted in Landon Jones, "The Baby Boomers," *Money,* March 1983, p. 58.
[2]Betty Friedan, *Second Stage* (New York: Summit Books, 1981), p. 47.
[3]Ibid., p. 49.
[4]Andrea Hinding, ed., *Feminism: Opposing Viewpoints* (St. Paul, Minn.: Greenhaven Press, 1986), p. 147.
[5]Friedan, *Second Stage,* p. 31.
[6]Ibid., p. 40.
[7]Sally Conway, *Women in Mid-Life Crisis* (Wheaton, Ill.: Tyndale House, 1987), p. 56.
[8]Gary Cartwright, "The Hungry Coach," *Texas Monthly,* September 1992, p. 107; Ed Hinton, "Deep into His Job," *Sports Illustrated,* September 7, 1992, p. 102.
[9]Tim Kimmel, *Little House on the Freeway* (Portland, Ore.: Multnomah Press, 1987), p. 31.
[10]Conway, *Women in Mid-Life Crisis,* p. 81.
[11]*Our Daily Bread* (Grand Rapids, Mich.: Radio Bible Class, 1992), entry for February 14, 1993.
[12]Ibid.
[13]Antoine de Saint-Exupéry as quoted in Tina Reed, ed., *Words of Love* (New York: Putnam, 1993), p. 55.

Chapter 5: The Pleasure of Forgiveness
[1]McKinney and Sprecher, *Sexuality in Close Relationships,* p. 63.
[2]Ibid., p. 65.
[3]Roache, "Premarital Sexual Attitudes," p. 119. This study found that in America we allow more freedom in what is deemed proper sexual behavior in others and less freedom in what is deemed proper in our own behavior.
[4]Isaiah 53:6 (New Century Version).
[5]Hebrews 8:12 (from Eugene H. Peterson, *The Message* [Colorado Springs, Colo.: NavPress, 1993], p. 467).
[6]Ephesians 1:7 *(The Message).*

Chapter 6: The Pleasure of Faithfulness
[1]Jeff Greenfield, "Babyboom Whitehouse," *USA Weekend,* January 15-17, 1993, p. 7.
[2]Jerry Jenkins, *Loving Your Marriage Enough to Protect It* (Chicago: Moody Press, 1989), p. 26, citing a *Christianity Today* survey taken for *Leadership,* Winter 1988, pp. 12-13.
[3]James Patterson and Peter Kim, *The Day America Told the Truth* (New York: Prentice-Hall, 1991), p. 97.
[4]Jenkins, *Loving Your Marriage Enough,* p. 27, citing Shere Hite, *The Hite Report on Male Sexuality* (New York: Knopf, 1981).
[5]Elaine Denholtz, *Having It Both Ways* (New York: Stein and Day, 1981), p. 223.

[6]Ibid., p. 226.

[7]"Feminist Follies," *Family Voice,* May 1993, p. 21, quoting *Good Morning America,* March 15, 1993.

[8]Helen Sanger Kaplan, *The New Sex Therapy* (New York: Brunner-Mazel, 1974), p. 159.

[9]Joseph Dillow, *Solomon on Sex* (Nashville: Thomas Nelson, 1977), p. 127.

[10]Samuel S. Janus and Cynthia L. Janus, "Janus Report on Sexual Behavior," *Redbook,* March 1993, p. 70.

[11]Ed Wheat and Gaye Wheat, *Intended for Pleasure* (Old Tappan, N.J.: Revell, 1980), p. 126.

[12]Janus and Janus, "Janus Report on Sexual Behavior," p. 114.

[13]Barna, *The Invisible Generation,* p. 139.

[14]Ibid., p. 145.

[15]Ibid.

[16]Willard F. Harley Jr., *Love Busters* (Tarrytown, N.Y.: Revell, 1992), p. 185.

[17]Patterson and Kim, *The Day America Told the Truth,* p. 97.

[18]Greeley, Michael and Smith, "Americans and Their Sexual Partners," p. 38.

[19]*The Oprah Winfrey Show,* ABC, April 14, 1993.

[20]Daniel Pearlman and Steve Duck, *Intimate Relationships* (Newbury Park, Calif.: Sage, 1987), p. 97.

[21]Michael Medved, "Hollywood Poison Factory: Making It a Dream Factory Again," *American Family Association Journal,* March 1993, p. 14.

[22]*Infosearch,* version 3.0 (Colorado Springs, Colo.: NavPress Software, 1987-1991.)

[23]Miriam and Otto Ehrenberg, *The Intimate Circle* (New York: Simon & Schuster, 1988), p. 57.

[24]Stephen Arterburn, *When Sex Becomes an Addiction* (Pomona, Calif.: Focus on the Family, 1991), p. 17.

[25]Conway and Conway, *When a Mate Wants Out.*

Chapter 7: The Pleasure of Authentic Desire

[1]Barbara DeAngelis, "Are You Sabotaging Your Sex Life?" *Family Circle,* January 12, 1993, p. 73.

[2]Grant L. Martin, "Relationship, Romance and Sexual Addiction in Extramarital Affairs," *Journal of Psychology and Christianity* 8, no. 4 (1989): 8.

[3]Ibid.

[4]Ibid., pp. 10-11.

[5]Elizabeth Cody Newenhuyse, "When the Thrill Is Gone," *Discipleship Journal* 64 (July/August 1991): 33.

[6]Amy Cunningham, "Married Sex," *McCall's,* May 1993, p. 74.

[7]Ibid.

[8]Ibid., p. 170.

[9]Harley, *Love Busters,* p. 213.

[10]Janice Irvine, *Disorders of Desire* (Philadelphia: Temple University Press, 1990), p. 12.

[11]Ibid., p. 117.

[12]Ibid., pp. 99, 120.

[13]Wheat and Wheat, *Intended for Pleasure,* pp. 239, 241.

[14]Pearlman and Duck, *Intimate Relationships,* p. 15.

[15]Lisa Hamilton, "Why We Need Passion," *Redbook*, February 1993, p. 68.

Chapter 8: The Pleasure of Self-Control
[1]Bob Phillips, *Powerful Thinking for Powerful Living* (Eugene, Ore.: Harvest House, 1991), p. 189.
[2]Gibb, *Twentysomething*, p. 127.
[3]Ibid., p. 58.
[4]Anonymous, "War Within," *Leadership*, Fall 1984, p. 41.
[5]Ibid.
[6]Gary L. Bauer, "Punching Out the Pornographers," *Citizen Magazine* 5, no. 10 (1991): 16.
[7]Ehrenberg and Ehrenberg, *The Intimate Circle*, p. 55.
[8]*Infosearch*.

Chapter 9: The Pleasure of Passion
[1]Dillow, *Solomon on Sex*, p. 21.
[2]Song of Songs 1:15.
[3]Song of Songs 2:2.
[4]Song of Songs 4:1.
[5]C. F. Keil and Franz Delitzsch, *Commentary on the Old Testament* (Grand Rapids, Mich.: Eerdmans, 1978), 6:72.
[6]Song of Songs 4:2-3.
[7]Christian Ginsburg, *Song of Songs* (New York: KTAV, 1970), p. 155.
[8]Song of Songs 4:3-4.
[9]Song of Songs 4:5.
[10]Dillow, *Solomon on Sex*, p. 76.
[11]Song of Songs 4:6.
[12]Dillow, *Solomon on Sex*, p. 77.
[13]Song of Songs 4:7-11.
[14]Song of Songs 4:12-14.
[15]Tim LaHaye, *How to Be Happy Though Married* (Wheaton, Ill.: Tyndale House, 1968), p. 64.
[16]Song of Songs 1:13.
[17]Keil and Delitzsch, *Commentary on the Old Testament*, 6:37.
[18]Song of Songs 1:14.
[19]S. Craig Glickman, *A Song for Lovers* (Downers Grove, Ill.: InterVarsity Press, 1976), p. 37.
[20]Song of Songs 2:6.
[21]Song of Songs 5:10-16.
[22]Dillow, *Solomon on Sex*, p. 114.
[23]Song of Songs 5:16
[24]Song of Songs 7:1-9.
[25]Song of Songs 7:11-12.

Chapter 10: The Pleasure of Fun
[1]Barna, *The Invisible Generation*, p. 137.

²Ibid., p. 140.

³Conway and Conway, *Women in Mid-Life Crisis,* p. 129.

⁴Conway and Conway, *When a Mate Wants Out,* p. 72.

⁵Interview with Jim and Sally Conway, "Can't You Hear What I Am Thinking?" *Marriage Partnership,* Winter 1993, p. 35.

⁶Conway, *Women in Mid-Life Crisis,* p. 112.

⁷Doug Fields, "Date Your Mate," *Focus on the Family,* February 1992, p. 3.

⁸Norman Wright, *Romancing Your Marriage* (Ventura, Calif.: Regal, 1987), p. 162.

⁹Charles Swindoll, *Laugh Again* (Wheaton, Ill.: Tyndale House, 1992), p. 192.

¹⁰Proverbs 17:22.

¹¹"Shorts," *Marriage Partnership,* Spring 1993, p. 11.

¹²Swindoll, *Laugh Again,* p. 103.

¹³Bob Phillips has pulled together many terrific clean joke books. They are all published by Harvest House, Eugene, Oregon: *The All American Joke Book, The All-New Clean Joke Book, The Best of the Good Clean Jokes, Bob Phillips' Encyclopedia of Good Clean Jokes* and *More Good Clean Jokes.*

¹⁴Wright, *Romancing Your Marriage,* p. 236.

¹⁵Doug Fields and Todd Temple, "How to Date Your Husband," *Partnership,* September/ October 1986, pp. 28-29.

¹⁶Ibid.

Chapter 11: The Pleasure of Decisiveness

¹Jim Conway, *Adult Children of Legal or Emotional Divorce* (Downers Grove, Ill.: Inter-Varsity Press, 1990), p. 128.

²Ibid., p. 130.

³Neil Anderson, *The Bondage Breaker* (Eugene, Ore.: Harvest House, 1990), p. 195.

⁴Don and Jan Frank, *When Victims Marry* (San Bernardino, Calif.: Here's Life, 1992), pp. 106-7.

⁵Ibid., p. 157.

⁶Personalized Scripture from Jeremiah 17:14 (LB); 1 Peter 5:7 (LB); Proverbs 3:5-6 (NASB); Psalm 147:3 (NASB); Psalm 107:13 (NASB).

Chapter 12: The Pleasure of Pure Love

¹1 Corinthians 6:19-20.

²See page 103.

³Conway and Conway, *Traits of a Lasting Marriage,* p. 37.

⁴Erik E. Filsinger and Margaret R. Wilson, "Religiosity, Socioeconomic Rewards and Family Development: Predictors of Marital Adjustment," *Journal of Marriage and the Family,* August 1984, p. 668. The authors found in a survey of Protestant church members in the Southwest that "religiosity was the most consistent and strongest predictor of marital adjustment." These researchers further discovered that the more involved a couple is in church and the more conservative their beliefs, the better the marital adjustment ("Religiosity and Marital Adjustment: Multidimensional Interrelationships," *Journal of Marriage and the Family,* February 1986, p. 149). David A. Martin found that those who attend church frequently are more likely to marry and less likely to divorce ("Religion and Public Values: A Catholic-Protestant Contrast," *Review of Religious Research,* June 1985,

p. 356).

[5]LaHaye and LaHaye, *The Act of Marriage*, introduction.

[6]Ibid., p. 223.

[7]Ephesians 5:21-33.

[8]Ephesians 5:33.

[9]In "God's Statement of Love to Us," all Scriptures quoted are from the *New Century Version* unless otherwise noted.

Appendix A: Activities to Deepen Your Pleasure

[1]James 1:5 (RSV). Also see Psalm 37:5-6; Proverbs 3:5-6; John 14:21; Romans 12:1-2; 1 Thessalonians 5:18.

[2]Ephesians 4:29 (NASB).

[3]Psalm 90:12.

[4]Galatians 2:20; 2 Corinthians 5:17; Ephesians 4:32 (NASB).

[5]1 Corinthians 10:13.

[6]See Genesis 2:24; Leviticus 18:5-23; Deuteronomy 24:5; Proverbs 5:18; Matthew 5:19; 19:5; Mark 7:21; 10:8; Romans 13:13; 1 Corinthians 5:1; 6:15-20; 7:2-6; Galatians 5:15-24; Ephesians 5:31; 1 Thessalonians 4:3.

[7]Hebrews 13:4.

[8]Philippians 4:8 (NASB).

[9]See Psalms 4:7; 16:11; 19:8; 21:6; 28:7; 30:11; 43:4; 51:12; 90:14; 92:4; 94:19.

[10]Tape titles: *Steve and Annie Chapman; Second Honeymoon; Circle of Two; Times and Seasons; Guest of Honor; Celebration of Womanhood; An Evening Together; The Greatest Gift; No Regrets; The Ships Are Burning.*

Appendix B: Resources for Recapturing Pleasure

[1]*Post-Abortion Syndrome*, available from Silent Voices, 191 Glover Ave., Suite B, Chula Vista, CA 91910.

[2]Ibid.

[3]NASAP brochure, available from Aaron J. Reinicke, 3430 Camino del Rio North, Suite 100, San Diego, CA 92108.

[4]Marilyn H. Stilson and Susan S. Hendrick, "Reported Childhood Sexual Abuse in University Counseling Center Clients," *Journal of Counseling Psychology* 39, no. 3 (1992): 370.

[5]Bob Burns and Tom Whiteman, *Fresh Start Divorce Recovery Workbook* (Nashville: Thomas Nelson, 1992), pp. 93, 97.

[6]Knud Larsen and Ed Long, "Attitudes Toward Rape," *The Journal for Sex Research* 24 (1988): 299.

[7]Patterson and Kim, *The Day America Told the Truth*, p. 129.

[8]Candace Walters, *Invisible Wounds* (Portland, Ore.: Multnomah Press, 1987), p. 45.

[9]Ibid., p. 59.

Bill and Pam Farrel

Bill and Pam have been counseling couples regarding sex and marriage since 1979. Bill has a masters degree from Biola University and has experience as a senior pastor, youth pastor, radio speaker, freelance writer and public speaker. Pam has a bachelor's degree in English and has experience as a director of women's ministry, youth leader, conference speaker and freelance writer. Pam has published articles in dozens of magazines and newspapers, including a Focus on the Family publication. They reside in southern California with their three sons, Brock, Zachery and Caleb.

Jim Conway, Ph.D., and Sally Christon Conway, M.S.

Jim and Sally are cofounders of Mid-Life Dimensions/Christian Living Resources, Inc., a California-based organization that offers help to people struggling to save or rebuild their marriages.

Jim and Sally speak together at colleges, seminaries, churches and retreat centers. They also appear on many radio and television programs. They previously were speakers on their own national daily radio program, *Mid-Life Dimensions*, broadcast on more than two hundred stations.

Jim served as a pastor for almost thirty years, while Sally served as pastor's wife. Sally also has been an elementary school remedial reading specialist. For five years Jim directed the Doctor of Ministry program at Talbot School of Theology, Biola University, and was associate professor of practical theology. Sally taught part-time at Talbot for five years.

Sally holds a Bachelor of Science degree in elementary education and a Master of Science degree in human development. Jim holds two earned doctorates—a D.Min. in ministry and a Ph.D. in adult development and learning.

Jim and Sally have three daughters, three sons-in-law and several grandchildren.

To contact them about speaking, write Bill and Pam Farrel at Masterful Living, 629 S. Rancho Santa Fe Rd., #306, San Marcos, CA 92069, or Jim and Sally Conway at Mid-Life Dimensions, P.O. Box 3790, Fullerton, CA 92634.